Where Did It All Go Wrong?

Adventures
At The
Dunning-Kruger
Peak Of
Advertising

EAON PRITCHARD

ART • SCIENCE • TECHNOLOGY

First published 2017
By ArtScienceTechnology
artsciencetechnology.com
P&D CreateSpace Independent Publishing
createspace.com
Copyright © 2017 Eaon Pritchard
ISBN-13: 978-1544901053

Maxine, Anthony and Hamish

Contents

Thanks.

To all those who have read, shared, commented and hurled abuse over the years. You know who you are.

And special thanks for foresight and inspiration goes to all the originators of the various ideas magpied and remixed in these pages. If I have seen further etc…(I haven't seen much further, but you know what I mean).

Foreword by Mark Earls

Back in the garage

It's hard to imagine now what it felt like being a teenager in '76-'77 when punk rock exploded in the UK. It was confusing and scary and exciting and liberating, all at the same time.

For years it seemed like we had only the choice between the languor of over-earnest singer-songwriters baring their souls to us, or the tedium of the five minute guitar solo which demanded adoration and an ability to fake enthusiasm in someone else's fantasy.

Music making was not something for the likes of us, surely?

Then along comes this swaggering cacophony of punk, breaking down the door. Suddenly, it was people like us - people we knew, even - making the music. Suddenly, it was as if the music mattered. Really mattered in a way that the *simpering* and the *stadium rockers* would never grasp.

Of course, every generation wants to feel this; every generation wants to kick over the traces of the previous generation's likes and loves. Every generation seems to want its own music - its own thing.

In time, of course, musical fashions changed. Punk faded (except for certain parts of NW1 and Chelsea's Kings Road) and then died (or at least, became no more than a genre to borrow from - you know who you are B****d and G**** D**).

But punk changed more than music: it shaped the attitudes of a generation.

It made music in particular, and culture more generally, a DIY thing. Go on, do it, punk said. Get up there. You can't sing? Never mind. Why not you on the mic? Who else is going to?

The other gift that punk gave us - the less easy to live with part - is the critical stance it taught us to take.

Don't trust those with power or those with a vested interest; don't believe a word those in authority tell you.

Don't let them pull the wool over your eyes.

Don't let them sidetrack you with the shiny stuff and the easy answers.

(And we're not going to fall for stuff - we're not selling out creatively or intellectually.)

'We're a garage band. We come from garage land' goes the shouty chorus of Garageland, the last song on the Clash's debut album.

This is where Eaon's book comes in; it's a rough and tumble challenge to any one who works in advertising and marketing.

A series of riffs which make us question the stuff we've been told about the jobs we do, and the things we make. It's garage band writing through and through.

Eaon's opinionated, sure. He's smart and well read, too.

But he's honest about where he makes mistakes and defiantly, stubbornly critical - he won't let you fall for the easy answer.

Each chapter is a lively essay on some aspect of the advertising and marketing world.

Each chapter takes some received wisdom and kicks it around the park a bit, like a can on the wet streets I remember from the 70s (no kids, it wasn't like an American Apparel ad), just to find the truth behind it.

Each chapter is like 2mins 22secs of raw energy to make you think again about some aspect of the business you thought you'd nailed.

If you're looking for a book with some magic formula, then this isn't for you.

But if you've had it up to here with the sickly sweet narcissism and embarrassing hollowness of the industry's conversation, if you want to start thinking critically again - punkily, even - about what it is you do for a living, then this is an excellent place to start.

And, oh, he has impeccable musical taste, too.

MARK EARLS
Bogotá, Colombia October 2017

Banging and shouting

John Walters described his relationship with John Peel as 'a bit like a master and his dog - each believing the other to be the dog'.

I've had similar relationships with a great many Creative Directors over the years. In most cases it was I who was master, obviously.

Walters, after a brief dalliance with pop stardom as trumpet player in the Alan Price Set in the late 60's, became producer of the John Peel radio show for the next 20 years or so.

During the mid-70's - during *punky* times - the pair would often check out the emerging and unsigned acts at London venues such as the 100 Club and The Roxy with a view to bringing in the new bands to record 'sessions' for the John Peel radio show.

On one such visit to the Oxford St basement that was - still is - the 100 Club, Walters and Peel encountered an early line-up of The Slits (an all-girl rarity on the nascent punk scene) and their chaotic mix of scratchy guitar, dub bass and clattering drums clicked with the dynamic duo.

So it goes, Walters and Peel eventually herded the girls into

Maida Vale and the resulting first Slits Peel session from September '77 still stands as one of the classic documents of the time. In describing the appeal of The Slits, Walters remarked that they represented - what he viewed to be - the very essence of punk.

'Banging and shouting...unhindered by any discernable musical ability'

In many respects this book mirrors much of that same quality as the early Slits. Banging and shouting, unhindered by talent.

But, hopefully, what it lacks in technique it makes up for in enthusiasm.

The Slits, and punk rock in general, are among a 'society' of memes that will crop up on a few occasions in this book.

The others are, principally, aspects of human psychology and contemporary advertising's identity crisis.

It was Richard Dawkins first coined the 'meme' meme in his 1976 book *The Selfish Gene*. If not 'coined' he certainly popularised the idea.

'Meme' describes an idea, behaviour or style that spreads from person to person within a 'culture'.

We love to talk about 'culture' in ad agencies. Often without knowing what we mean. There are at least two principle manifestations of culture.

The first is what we might describe as 'transmitted culture'. Representations, beliefs or ideas that originally exist in one (or more) minds and are spread to other minds through observation or interaction. These are memes.

It's worth remembering that evoked culture is just as influential. Universal evolved mechanisms responding in different ways to differing environmental conditions. More on that later.

Most proto-memes go nowhere and are quickly forgotten, or are not noticed at all. However, some memes find a tipping point of sorts - and spread - increasing in momentum as they go. These ideas are often described as the ones that 'go critical'.

Some memes need to mutate to persevere; others can propagate by 'hitch-hiking' on the back of other ideas.

For example, around the same time that Dawkins was finalising 'The Selfish Gene', Bernie Rhodes was managing The Clash and meme-building in cahoots with Malcolm McLaren (Sex Pistols) and Jake Riviera (the unsung 3rd man of the original UK punk scene, and manager of The Damned).

Between the three of them they realised that to create a movement - and the 'meme' of punk rock - some initial *momentum* needed to be created. One band could not do it on its own, but 3 bands could hitchhike with each other...

Do the arithmetic.

We have 3 bands (Pistols, Clash, Damned) each with four members. Say each band member has five 'friends', that's 60 people minimum. So a triple-header gig in a small strip joint in Soho has an instant crowd of 60 or so like-minded freaks, therefore to any waif or stray that has wandered in off the street it immediately looks like 'something' is happening.

As more people decide to join in it's no longer a risk for hesitant onlookers, and the *codes, language, and style* are all there for them to pick up. And punk 'goes critical'. Then the door opened for the likes of The Slits.

I get a sense that some concern, a proto-meme, for where advertising appears to be heading is beginning to 'go critical', there are now a significant number of commentators and practitioners taking stock and realising that we went off the rails somewhere. This meme is not yet fully formed, its still mutating into full fitness. Perhaps some of what follows in this book will contribute to the debate.

Of course, meme 'fitness' is not dependent on the meme itself having any properties of good 'quality'. It just needs an environment that increases *replicability*.

At the time of writing one particular meme that begins with 'Amazon didn't kill the retail industry...they did it to themselves with bad customer service' and then goes on to list a host of other industries, taxis, music, hotels, Blockbuster video and so on, that are apparently 'dead' from non customer-centricity, has replicated itself successfully around the internet despite being complete horseshit.

None of those 'dead' things are dead, of course, apart from Blockbuster, which was a brand rather than a category in any case, and the reasons for its demise are most likely to be far more to do with a multitude of other boardroom factors invisible to the average Linked-In or Twitter ranter.

The meme is *selected for* in a *Dunning Kruger* environment.

However, one industry is in danger of serious injury, if not death, from a variety of *malaise* (including lack of customer-centricity) and that is the advertising business.

That's the broad theme of this book, as we try to figure out where it all went wrong.

I'm not certain we will find any solutions - there's a lot that needs fixing - but I can almost certainly guarantee plenty of *banging and shouting*.

A couple of final caveats to end this intro.

Firstly, if I'm critical of what advertising has become it's only because I love it, and I want it to be better.

Secondly, returning the aforementioned 'lack of discernable

talent'. Well, I've read loads of books so it obviously follows that I should be able to write one.

Applied logical fallacies aside, to wait around for the time to be 'right' before doing something means a very long wait because, unfortunately, that day never comes.

Until then I'm going to fake it 'til I make it.

In an early episode of David Simon's classic HBO crime drama, *The Wire*, rival drug gangs from Baltimore's Eastside and Westside leave their guns at home for a day and clash on the basketball court.

Eastside 'coach' Prop Joe – a 'nice' drug boss, he preferred to settle inter-gang disputes by peaceful means, hence the basketball match - is called out by his Westside counterpart, Avon Barksdale, for his choice of attire, an expensive suit.

Avon asks, 'How come you wearin' that suit? Its 85 fuckin' degrees outside and you tryin' to be like Pat Riley'.

Joe responds, 'Look the part - be the part, motherfucker!'

Lobotomy

I regard sleep as an essential part of my work.

At the moment I'm interested in 90-minute sleep cycles. 90mins is the optimum cycle, this means that you should, in theory, feel more refreshed after 3 hours sleep than after 5 - waking after 5 hours means you have woken mid-cycle.

The psychologist Richard Wiseman says a good sleep is like a cycle on a washing machine - cleaning out your mind of the day's memories that you don't need.

We all receive vast amounts of information during the day, and quite a lot of it - campaign tracker research reports, for example - can be totally useless, so this sorts out which memories are important and which to discard.

A good way of distracting the mind and getting off to sleep is by imagining positive scenarios. Perhaps this quietens the mind (you can trick yourself into believing you have achieved something in life). In any case, I've come across many marketers who must be able to sleep very easily by using this technique.

They are especially adept at building fantasy worlds in their head and should be able to drift off easily with very positive imagery of successful loyalty programs, social media engagement metrics, passionate brand advocates and suchlike.

At home, I try and park work stuff into my subconscious as much as possible and let it sort itself out while I'm doing other things.

Discerning creatives will be familiar with the seminal 1939 work by James Webb Young, entitled *A Technique for Producing Ideas.*

In stage 3 of his 5-step process Young outlines the benefits of removing the particular problem you are trying to solve from your conscious mind in order to stimulate the unconscious mind.

For readers familiar with Kahneman-isms, this method is akin to giving your *system two* processes a rest and allowing *system one* processes to do the heavy lifting.

Young likens this to how Sherlock Holmes would often stop right in the middle of a case, and drag Watson off to a cello recital, or something.

That was always vexatious to the more hardboiled Watson, but letting the unconscious grapple with a problem was essential to the creative process for Holmes.

This stuff is important if one has to think for a living.

Deliberate thinking for 8 or 10 hours a day can be pretty draining. It's easy to understand why your brain will avoid it if at all possible. Because your brain is a physical system.

And your mind is what your brain *does.*

Using the mind, the brain processes information by thinking (fast and slow), it's a kind of computation.

Although the brain-as-computer metaphor has been retired in recent years, computational theory of mind still holds. We'll discuss that a bit later on, but suffice to say many neuro experts are now talking about the brain as like the ultimate *mobile device*, and consequently a *brain-as-iphone* metaphor is perhaps a better model to work with.

This thinking is based on an idea popularised by the evolutionary psychologists Leda Cosmides and John Tooby who proposed that the brain is the hardware and the mind is software - or a suite of apps if you prefer. Each app a discrete, domain-specific mental module.

Cosmides and Tooby suggest that these modules are units of mental processing that evolved at different times in response to selection pressures in our ancestral past.

Steven Pinker, another psychologist this author refers to on a daily basis (and you'll see bits and pieces of his wisdom peppered liberally throughout the rest of this book), captures this idea nicely in his book *How The Mind Works*.

> 'The mind is organized into modules or mental organs, each with a specialized design that makes it an expert in one arena of interaction with the world...a system of organs of computation, designed by natural selection to solve the kinds of problems our ancestors faced in their foraging way of life, in particular, understanding and out-manoeuvring objects, animals, plants, and other humans.'

The *iphone* metaphor works just fine, as long as we understand that there is a lot more interaction between the mind's *apps* than the apps on your phone. Sometimes in order to collaborate, but mostly to compete for control of the organism. And, most importantly, these apps activate themselves in response to the environment rather than requiring the actions of a user.

There's a Darwinian logic to this metaphor. Early human minds started off with a few basic apps, and as humans faced new environmental challenges, new apps would have been added over time.

So whilst we humans possess all the necessary hardware and the software for serious thinking, not all living things even need brains.

Trees, flowers and other plants, for example, don't have brains. Things that don't move tend not to have brains.

In fact, there are also some animals that don't move during stages of their lives, and during those stages, they don't have brains either.

One such creature is the Sea Squirt. A small aquatic animal that inhabits shallow waters and reefs in many parts of the world. During the early stage of its life cycle, and using its rudimentary brain, the sea squirt swims around looking for a good rock to attach itself to, permanently.

The creature needs to find somewhere with a good passing supply of food, principally plankton and organic matter that they strain from the water they pump through their bodies. Once it finds the right rock, and attaches itself to it, the creature doesn't need its brain anymore. All the hard work has been done and it will never need to think again. So, now it eats its own brain.

This phenomenon - if not unique - is at least extraordinarily rare. In fact, outside of marine biology, the only other environment where this behaviour seems to occur with any frequency in the natural world is in the world of business, and advertising agencies in particular.

These environments are host to large numbers of people who have found a nice desk at which to attach themselves and appear to have given up on thinking, or at least letting in *critical thinking*.

This is all a bit disappointing if, like me, you are one of the people who still believe in the power of human creativity to solve our biggest business problems.

Because, and as evolutionary theory has taught us, we humans are fairly unique among species. We haven't evolved adaptations like huge fangs, inch-thick armour plating or the ability to move at super speed under our own steam.

All of the big adaptations have happened inside our heads. The principle *amelioration* has been these huge brains we carry around. Giant *iphones* full of *killer apps* built for creativity and sussing out how the world works.

But most days if feels like we left them at home. As the saying goes, stupidity is often in the eye of the beholder, and some have bad eyesight.

Maybe we've lost a bit of the art of scepticism. Being sceptical is not just about being the naysayer or debunker, although for those who are overly attached to the kinds of concepts to which scepticism is best applied - ghosts, the Loch Ness monster or content marketing, for example - then it may appear that way.

Contemporary scepticism is a process of evaluating claims, not a set of conclusions. It's a scientific method. Indeed, the key tenet of scepticism is that any extraordinary claims will require extraordinary evidence to back them up. If we're expected to revise or overturn well-established knowledge, or take on supernatural explanations, it is not unreasonable to ask for this. Science is the ultimate bullshit detector. And as we are living in an era of *peak bullshit* it's the best tool we have.

This author may have even eaten his own brain once up on a time but he hopes that a least some of this document is a sign that a brain can *grow back*. A bit.

Enough, at least, to attempt to navigate the perennial functional stupidity that prevails in this industry, and to summon the necessary *puissance* in order to keep going forward, and maybe pick up a few others on the way.

It's going to be tough. No one is good at multitasking, particularly the kind of multitasking that requires keeping an open mind with the bullshit detector running concurrently.

Author Terry Pratchett once insightfully remarked that the trouble with having an open mind is that other people will insist on trying to put things in it!

For the rest of this book we'll try to ensure that the arguments follow *Dennett's rules* as much as possible - aiming to encourage productive, critical discourse and avoid straw man representations - and as the great man said 'unless you are a comedian whose main purpose is to make people laugh at ludicrous buffoonery, spare us the caricature'.

More cheap philosophy as we go. But for now, follow me down, as we embark on this wonderful yet frightening journey to the Dunning Kruger Peak of advertising…

You know me I'm acting dumb

'But I wore the juice!'

As Charles Darwin famously offered, ignorance more frequently begets confidence than does knowledge. And never has this insight revealed itself more clearly than in the curious case of one McArthur Wheeler.

Wheeler was a man who, in 1995, proceeded to rob two banks in Pittsburgh, Pennsylvania - in broad daylight - expecting to avoid detection by simply covering his face with lemon juice.

You see, Wheeler had read somewhere that lemon juice is a principle ingredient in the manufacture of 'invisible' ink.

Bingo.

Clearly, by applying the juice he could render his own face completely invisible to the surveillance cameras, and commit the perfect crime. Wheeler was double confident in this belief as he had tested the hypothesis by taking a proto-selfie with a Polaroid camera and the result had presented an image of only the bare wall. No face!

The juice had done it.

His face was completely invisible. So it seemed.

Unfortunately he had simply aimed his shot badly.

Needless to say, it was all downhill from there. He was nicked and behind bars within a couple of hours.

The story inspired the psychologists David Dunning and Justin Kruger from the Department of Psychology at Cornell University to conduct some experiments. Their results were published in 1999, in the landmark study *Unskilled and Unaware Of It.*

In a nutshell, the two Professors subsequent thesis was this.

If you're incompetent, you can't know you're incompetent because the skills you would need to produce a right answer are exactly the skills you lack in order to know what a right answer is.

This observation became established in the psychology canon as the *Dunning-Kruger Effect.*

A more everyday manifestation of the phenomenon can be seen in the hapless yet strangely confident performances featured in the likes of Britain's Got Talent, The X Factor and other TV talent shows. In particular the auditions shows in which incompetent individuals mistakenly rate their abilities much higher than is strictly accurate.

For the talent show hopefuls, the sweet Mariah Carey tones

that they hear inside their own heads unfortunately bear no resemblance to the hideous cacophonies actually coming out of their mouths.

Part of the problem is the fact that none of the people around our untalented and unaware subjects - family, friends, and colleagues - are prepared to tell them the truth.

These people, while well intentioned, can be reasonably described as *mediocrity enablers* and therefore the delusion becomes even more entrenched.

Conversely, many people who actually DO possess some skill or talent tend to underestimate their own talent, and wrongly assume that things that are easy for them to do are also easy for others. Insecure ad planners, this is you lot.

As Dunning and Kruger famously note, 'the miscalibration of the incompetent stems from an error about the self, whereas the miscalibration of the highly competent stems from an error about others'

Anyway, by now you will start to see how this is leading us into the crazy world of advertising.

There is a point, often labelled the Dunning-Kruger *peak,* that represents the particular surge of self-confidence one gets upon acquiring a small amount of skill in a field. It represents the huge leap from *total novice to semi-skilled amateur.*

However the deluded amateur, at this stage both encouraged their new found knowledge yet unable to know the vastness of what they have yet to learn in order to be an expert, begin to imagine themselves to actually *be* expert.

This period of delusion is common in people who are just starting out in advertising. Based on scant evidence, and perhaps one too many Gary Vaynerchuck videos - although there's plenty to learn from Gary V on *delivery*, to be fair - ad youth tend to believe they are much more knowledgeable about advertising than they actually are.

In fairness to the kids, this is understandable and excusable to some extent. As my fellow countryman J. M. Barrie - most famous for penning *Peter Pan* - wrote for the character Ernest Woolley in *The Admirable Crichton* in 1902.

'I am not young enough to know everything'.

Moreover, and more worryingly, this delusion seems to also envelope entire groups, and beleaguers people with enough experience to know much better, which is why I suggest that a part of our industry appears to have hit some sort of Dunning-Kruger peak.

The commonly held ideas of those operating in Dunning-Kruger peak mode are some sort of party-mix of the following.

'Advertising is dead, everything is now about participation and conversation', 'creative departments are no longer required as ideas come from anywhere', 'user experience design will be all about anti-open source hyper-telling in a world defined by uncertainty' and how 'winning responsive organisations create digital-darwinistic content amplification as a service' and many others.

Ok, the last two were quoted directly from the @*DouchebagStrategist* planner-gobbledygook twitter bot, but certainly sound plausible enough as examples of the kind of nonsense that can be read in the industry press and spoken onstage at industry events.

Joking aside, a not entirely unexpected by-product of Dunning Kruger peak era advertising is an equivalent peak in the production of bullshit.

In [adland] the bullshit piled so high you needed wings to stay above it.

(Never get out of the boat. Absolutely goddam right.)

As the philosopher Harry Frankfurt, whom we shall consult again later, famously noted.

'Bullshit is unavoidable whenever circumstances require someone to talk without knowing what [he] is talking about. Thus the production of bullshit is stimulated whenever person's obligations or opportunities to speak about some topic exceed his knowledge of the facts that are relevant to that topic.

This discrepancy is common in [advertising agencies], where people are frequently impelled - whether by their own propensities or by the demands of others - to speak extensively about matters of which they are to some degree ignorant.'

So our main protagonists, Dunning and Kruger, discovered that people who are unskilled at something - in our case, advertising - are often unable to see how bad they really are.

Incompetent people will...

Fail to recognise that they are incompetent, fail to recognise how good competent people actually are and also fail to see the scale of their own incompetence.

How do I know this?

Well, to an extent this story is my own story.

Armed with Twitter and grab bag of Seth Godin one-liners (no disrespect to Seth intended, he's written some splendid stuff although we do diverge on his advertising-industrial complex thesis) I spent a number of years parroting much of the standard social media douchebag drivel, and having a reasonably successful career to boot, until eventually having a moment of true insight when I realised exactly how incompetent I actually was.

To be truthful, there was no one moment of clarity. There

was more of a procedure akin to that described by the _Sorites_ _Paradox_. A peeling away.

1000 tons of bullshit is a heap of bullshit, 1000 tons minus one ton is still a heap of bullshit.

I do give some credit to a kindly Brand Manager who first passed me a copy of Byron Sharp's _How Brands Grow_, hot off the press sometime in 2010. I'd been wheeled out to the headquarters of a global FMCG company to give one of my signature 'the sky is falling' presentations on social media marketing and the death of mass advertising.

To my dismay the talk was met with stony silence and blank expressions from the gathered marketers and product people. As I hastily made my exit, the aforementioned Brand Manager informed me, 'Eaon, all this stuff is very entertaining but you will get nowhere with these people taking like that. They're only interested in the science and evidence. And you don't have any'.

She stuffed the book into my bag as I left and told me to come back when I'd read it and understood.

I've not been back, but I hope to fare better next time if I do get another invite.

Suffice to say, over time enough scientific rabbit holes were explored and layers of bullshit were removed and your author tumbled from his Dunning-Kruger Peak into a trough of enlightened ignorance where he began to realise that the things he didn't know massively outnumbered the things he'd learned. In photographer lingo this is 'the Jon Snow trough', named after a character in *Game of Thrones,* apparently.

On the upside, despite being dumped in the trough, one is now actually skilled to some degree yet saddled with the tendency to underestimate one's own skill when compared to the over confident noises made by the mass of incompetents. Imposter syndrome! It never stops.

But as another great philosopher, Rocky Balboa, once remarked. 'It's not about how hard you hit, it's about how hard you can GET HIT and still keep comin' back'.

For the adperson to hasten their *aggiornamento*, one important insight - and one that is best absorbed sooner rather than later - comes from realising that the consumers we have to communicate with spend precious little time thinking about brands, do next to no evaluation around most purchase decisions, and even brands that they use and like are trivial in comparison to the rest of their daily lives.

Rather than engagement, conversations or participation people's actual buying behaviour is about reducing complexity, reducing choice and making easier, good-enough decisions.

Our job is simply about getting brands noticed, remembered at the appropriate time and then bought.

Just getting that teeny tiny bit of attention needed is hard enough, never mind all the other bollocks.

Of course there is an inverse of the Dunning Kruger effect. Another cognitive blind spot, sometimes called the 'curse of knowledge'.

In this case, and having clawed oneself out of the *trough*, you experience a difficulty in imagining what it is like for someone else not to know what you now know and mistakenly assuming that the knowledge and skills one has finally acquired are obvious to everyone else, too.

Like the fella once said, 'Never make predictions, particularly about the future'

Perhaps a wish, then.

A wish that, sooner rather than later, all of us in the business of marketing communications - of all flavours - fall from our Dunning-Kruger peak, and recognise that while we do have some skills and influence, what we don't know about communications and human behaviour is so much more than what we do know. A good place to start is addressing one's own stupidity first, not the stupidity of others.

It's not easy. As Dr Dunning says:

'The trouble with ignorance is that it **feels** so much like expertise'.

Dumbo dynamics

It looks like efficiency.

There's no shortage of bluster on the next 'new agency model' or (at least) semi-ignorant Dunning-Kruger advice on 'why advertising is broken and how to fix it'.

Ignorance that looks like expertise.

I've no desire to add anything much to that tedious narrative other than to add that there is no 'new agency model' - most agencies will operate in multiple different ways with different clients and often running a variety of models simultaneously.

What we wish to outline here, is a common problem *within* agencies of *all* flavours - be they 'new model' or otherwise.

And it's nothing to do with the *fragmentation of media, consumers-in-control, the collaborative economy* or *how a digestible content strategy will eat advertising*.

Nor is it in anyway connected to the *rise of influencers, purpose-before-profit* or *branded communities of millennials demanding marketing from the spirit and psychic satisfaction*.

That last one is from Philip Kotler and his 'Marketing 3.0'

manifesto. Reader beware - its not satire.

No, by far and away the biggest problem in agencies is that people don't know when to keep their mouths shut, and don't know when to speak up.

And then do both of those things at the wrong times.

Frank Black spoke about the Pixies much imitated quiet-loud song structure dynamic. 'We do try to be dynamic, but it's dumbo dynamics, because we don't know how to do anything else. We can play loud or quiet - that's it'.

Frank's dumbo dynamics description is excessively modest. Knowing exactly *when* to play loud and *when* to play quiet is no small accomplishment. Muddling quiet-loud can kill a song.

Real dumbo dynamics, or *Dunning-Kruger effects*, can be found in advertising agencies.

The first dumbo dynamic is when people can't keep their mouths shut when they should be saying nothing.

To illustrate this, lets call up something from popular culture, a scene from Coppolla's 1972 classic *The Godfather*.

It's Don Vito Corleone's daughter Connie's wedding day, and Santino 'Sonny' Corleone is in a clandestine meeting with Virgil 'The Turk' Sollozzo in which they discuss a potential opportunity for the Corleones in Sollozzo's nascent heroin business, which he plans to bring to New York.

(This discussion is happening without Don Vito Corleone's prior knowledge and ultimately leads to the attempt on the Don's life later on…)

Sonny is already receptive to the heroin idea; narcotics look likely to be a lucrative business in the near future and worth getting into, early on.

Sonny sets up a meeting with Sollozzo, Tom Hagen - the Corleone's consigliore (who is similarly enthusiastic) - and the still reluctant Don.

Sollozzo arrives in New York and has already 'secretly' allied with the rival Tattaglia family on the heroin venture, however his strategy still requires bringing in the Corleone family for further financial backing (and because the Don has the cops and justice departments in his pocket).

Don Vito - unbeknown to Sollozzo - is already wise to the Tattaglia involvement and decides to decline the offer on the basis that heroin is generally a bad business and - in any case - involvement would put unnecessary strain his political connections, which he viewed as strategically more valuable in the long game.

During Vito's polite refusal of Sollozzo's offer, Sonny - incensed by Sollozzo's faintly ridiculous suggestion that the Tattaglias could be relied on to guarantee the Corleones investment - breaks ranks and interrupts his father with a display of temper directed at Sollozzo.

Vito calmly puts Sonny back in his box, and once their guests have departed expresses his disappointment with Sonny's indiscretion.

'Never tell anyone outside the family what you're thinking again'.

The damage has been done, unfortunately.

Sollozzo now knows a few things that he didn't know before. Sonny (Vito's eldest son, family underboss and therefore next in line to the throne) is:

a) More receptive to the heroin idea

b) Prepared to speak over the top of Vito and

c) Unable to keep his cool in a business situation.

The Turk now starts to think that a good strategy would be to take out Don Vito and enable the ascent of the weaker Sonny to *Capo*.

Sonny's outburst not only undermined the Don but also undermined the credibility of the entire Corleone family and sowed the seeds for a whole lot of pain down the road.

As it transpires this mistake does start a cascade of misfortune for the family - including the death of Sonny - and

Don Vito capitulating. He buys into the heroin business against his better judgement in a compromise move designed to prevent an all-out war among the crime families.

Slightly less dramatically, many years ago I was a designer in a small but emerging agency.

The founders had a lot to say for themselves; a definite point of view on the world and it was an exciting, if sometimes *seat-of-the-pants*, ride.

One Friday afternoon a junior client called up and asked the account person if we could make a small change to some element of an ad.

This was right at the last minute before the thing was due out of the door.

Both the Creative Director and the Planning Director were out so the account person agreed, instructed me to make the change, the ad went off and that was that.

Later that evening I got a message from the Planning Director indicating we would be having a chat on the Monday morning.

By 'chat' it became clear that he meant getting the metaphorical shit kicked out of me by him and the CD.

By making - what seemed to me to be minor - changes to the ad on the request of a junior client, without consulting the

CD, I had undermined the credibility of the entire agency. I had made us look like we didn't know what we were doing.

I learned something that day.

Several years and several agencies later I sat in a presentation to a new marketing team at a long-time client. The ECD was presenting our latest iteration of a long-running campaign.

At the end of the show the new marketing chief started making some commentary on the work and suggesting small changes to the copy, art direction and suchlike.

The ECD sat stony faced while receiving the feedback and then removed the work from the table explaining that if the client didn't like the idea then we would take it away and come back with something else.

The marketer wouldn't be put off, insisting that by incorporating just a few of his changes the work would be fine.

To which the ECD responded, 'Thank you Mr. [name], but we'll come back with another idea. I don't tell you how to make [the product] so please don't tell me how to make advertising'.

That might look like arrogance to some, it probably was, but to me this felt just about necessary. Because I knew that the creative credibility of the agency must be preserved, almost at all costs.

This is not about stroking creative egos. I have had many a stand-up row with CDs over the years. It's the planner's job to make sure the advertising is 'right'.

For one's own credibility that means being prepared to scrap. However, those things happen behind closed doors. It doesn't matter how much I disagree with a Creative Director I would never voice that in a client situation or any other situation where their status could be undermined.

Bob Hoffman says that 'everyone else in an agency are organisers, and the creatives make the ads'.

This is right to a certain extent, but most certainly should be the impression given to people from 'outside'.

Agencies are judged by their creative output.

When non-creatives undermine the creative product - by unquestioningly acquiescing to client whims or making their own suggestions in the presence of anyone outside of the agency - it undermines the entire agency.

The popular notion of 'ideas can come from anywhere' is in part to blame. Of course ideas can come from anywhere, however that does not make them good ideas. Good commercial creativity tends to come from people who's job it is to have these ideas. If they don't come up with the goods then they won't last very long in the creative department.

The rest of us can help *improve* ideas, for sure. But those conversations have to happen behind closed doors. When you devalue the agency's creative ideas in public, you capitulate. When you devalue ideas, you undermine the whole agency.

Reputations take a long time to build but can be shot very quickly. And it's a long way back.

That's dumbo dynamic number one. Dumbo dynamic number two occurs when people say nothing when they should be speaking up.

You have met these folks. These are the 'quiet fixers'.

Good soldiers whom, quietly and without fuss, fix things that are broken.

The simple reason why this is a big problem is because no one even notices that it's a problem.

In fact, it looks like efficiency.

A problem arises; someone notices it, applies some little 'fix' and moves on with minimal disruption to anything else going on, and no one needs to know.

Why is this such a big deal?

'Jidoka', is a Japanese term, more specifically a principle from the *Toyota Production System*. Roughly translated it means autonomation, or 'automation with a human touch'. A type of automation that allows workers to apply supervisory functions to automated systems. Automation and autonomy.

At Toyota this usually means that if an abnormal situation arises in the production process, the worker stops the machine and the production line, to investigate. It is part of the quality control process that applies the following four principles.

- Detect the abnormality.

- Stop.

- Fix or correct the immediate condition.

- Investigate the root cause and install a countermeasure.

Everything stops until the problem is figured out.

Why does this matter?

Let's ask ex-Toyota chairman Katsuaki Watanabe.

'Hidden problems are the ones that become serious threats eventually. If problems are revealed for everyone to see, I will feel reassured.

Because once problems have been visualized, even if our people didn't notice them earlier, they will rack their brains to find solutions to them.

In Toyota, if a problem is noticed, production on the line stops, the entire team comes together to identify the root cause of the problem, to ensure it does not happen again.'

Quiet Fixers cause two principle problems.

Type 1.

Even if the quiet fixer solves a genuine issue then the rest of us never get the chance to know that it was a problem - therefore the root cause never gets addressed and in all likelihood that exact same problem will come up again in the future.

But worse (and sadly, more common)

Type 2.

The quiet fixer 'solves' a problem that wasn't even a real problem in the first place and therefore creates a problem.

These Type 2 quiet fixes normally happen further down the line of production, and usually begin with the words 'can you just...' followed by 'move that button', 'make it red' or 'change that word to...'

To the fixer it may even feel like they're doing the right thing. To the fixer these 'asks' can seem like mere trivialities, minor no-harm-done tweaks that may perhaps appease a client.

I've always liked what the great philosopher and best-dressed fictional New York law firm boss, Harvey Specter, says about client relations. 'We're not here to make clients happy, we're here to make them succeed.'

Rory Sutherland once remarked on the (then) growing influence of decision science and behavioural economics in advertising practice:

> 'Unfortunately, [the] science is probably closer to being climatology in that in many cases, very, very small changes can have disproportionately huge effects'

But it can go the other way, and it's these small problems - quietly 'fixed' or hidden by inexperienced hands – that can do serious damage to a piece of communication, or to how a thing works, and may only get discovered when it's too late.

Hiding problems undermines everyone. We are supposed to learn from our mistakes.

One of the major reasons that we never learn is that because when something goes wrong, the first thing we do is look for ways of covering it up. Then we make the same mistake over and over.

Or as the Toyota massive say; 'No problem' *IS* a problem'.

Of course people usually want to do the right thing. But if it isn't possible to speak up and get the job done effectively, they will choose to get the job done and keep quiet.

Maybe there is not a good system in your agency for helping people to do the right thing.

A 'tell' in poker is when a player's behaviour or demeanour

gives clues to that player's assessment of their hand.

A Dunning-Kruger 'tell' in advertising is when we don't train our people on when to keep their mouths shut, and then when to speak up - and, even worse, get those occasions the wrong way round.

Showing our hand when it is not a good hand, even though it looks like efficiency.

Instead its just agency dumbo dynamics.

'Shh shh,
It's nice and quiet,
But soon again,
Starts another big riot!'

Where did it all go wrong?

'A bag of money never scored a goal'.

According to legend, one night in late 1974, ex-Manchester United soccer superstar star and Belfast's most famous sporting export, George Best, had just spent a very successful evening in the casino accompanied by the reigning Miss World.

They had just won a silly amount of money - around 15,000GBP (that's close to a hundred grand in today's money) - brought it back to their hotel room and ordered up a magnum of the hotel's best champagne which was shortly delivered by an Irish room service waiter.

The waiter looked at George, looked at Miss World, the piles of cash surrounding the pair all over the bed. The champagne was popped and before leaving the waiter famously asked…

"So tell me now George…where did it all go wrong?"

Our waiter's typically dark Belfast humour aside, on the surface George certainly didn't look like he had too many problems, but something, somewhere had fundamentally gone wrong for world soccer's first superstar.

Whether this particular casino story is exactly true or not is not important. What *is* true is that even as early 1971 George's hectic off-field celebrity lifestyle was widely believed to be reducing his effectiveness on the pitch.

That was the popular view but perhaps also true was that the slow, steady decline of Manchester United's status and fortunes since the departure from the dressing room of legendary coach Matt Busby was taking its toll on George's enthusiasm for the game.

In just a couple of years following the spectacular European Cup win of '68 the ageing United had effectively become a one-man show, George was carrying the whole team.

That alternative explanation is worth its inclusion. This is a book that is principally about advertising, after all. And if there's one thing that has remained constant over time is our ability to consistently get cause and effect the wrong way round.

Either way, whilst arguably the most talented footballer of his generation, or just about any other subsequent generation, the wayward Best was now rapidly developing a reputation for general unreliability and regularly going AWOL rather than participating in training sessions.

And he was now even missing matches.

This erratic behaviour coincided with Best's developing problems with alcoholism and he eventually parted company with his beloved United (and football) during the 1973/74 season, at the end of which the once mighty Manchester giants were relegated to the second tier of the English Football League.

George was only 27 when he quit - an age when most players are usually regarded as being at or near their peak - and without the distraction of football George was now free to pursue his other principal interests; those being the aforementioned drinking, gambling and the company of glamorous women.

The notion of a self-fulfilling prophecy is often over-used and over-stated.

Ideas that become reality simply because an individual believes them do not usually turn out and, despite the claims of the self-help book industry - and as Sean Bean would concur - one does not just simply think oneself rich.

But there is something to be said for how expectations may come to pass when many people hold the same beliefs. George's boozy exploits, alongside the 'wasted genius that threw it all away' narrative were never far from the tabloid headlines. So believe it, we did.

If we follow the money, then the advertising business would

appear to be in rude health in 2017.

Global ad spending is said to be growing faster than at anytime in the digital era. The most recent eMarketer Worldwide Adspend Forecast estimates that total spending is will reach around $725 billion (USD) by 2020. That's growth of between 5% to 9% year on year, with digital and mobile spend contributing to about 36% of that at present, growing to nearly half by 2020. Big bucks.

And the glamour?

For George Best the continuous company of a sequence of Miss World winners ticked that box while the Rosé-fuelled, celebrity splattered and yacht propelled Cannes Festival is our thing.

These extravagant festivals are not going away anytime soon, however, many influential agency types are starting to question the value they create.

For some, Cannes has become a parody. Tom Goodwin calls it a 'self-serving fetishisation of the newly possible and the highly improbable'. Yet also predictable and formulaic awash with novelty technology for it's own sake and about as far from the everyday concerns of the average shopper as it is possible to be.

It's hard not to agree with that point of view - at least in part - when observing some of the winning entries from 2017.

Much of the silliness seemed to abound in the 'Innovation' category, of course.

Awarding a Gold Lion for a Grand Theft Auto 5 mod seems like a bit of a stretch, while the Innovation Grand Prix was awarded to a smelting project for recycling handguns.

What these activities have to do with brand communications is anyone's guess, but they are symptomatic of the real and bigger problems for this industry that are only now starting to unravel.

There's money all over the bed, but pull back the covers and there's a horse's head.

We'll never know for sure, but when the horse's head was attached to its body the whole horse almost certainly hated advertising.

These days everybody seems to hate it.

It's not just those cheeky 'authenticity-seeking purpose-driven millennials' that claim to hate advertising. Even 'old' people (that's over 45's in ad speak, btw) will say they hate it, while the advertising and marketing trade press definitely hates it.

And lastly, most of the people who work in advertising and media agencies seem to hate their jobs and hate the idea that they are selling brands, products and services rather than the

47

more noble aim of solving society's problems.

> 'Our best trained, best educated, best equipped, best prepared troops refuse to fight. As a matter of fact, it's safe to say that they would rather…switch, than fight!'

With apologies to Chuck D and Thomas N Todd, maybe it's more charitable to say that we've now 'successfully' produced a generation of advertising professionals who have never even known what advertising is for and how it works.

And who's going to teach them? Well, the rest of us appear to have completely forgotten.

Being even a bit more cynical we may say we've turned a business that used to value ideas and creativity into 'a pig's breakfast of insufferable bullshit, dreadful jargon, stupid gimmicks, and amateur bumblers producing horrific crap', to use a classic Hoffman-ism.

Who needs creativity when you can be *'growth-hacking a well-integrated purpose and empowering organizational pivots in order to navigate today's disrupted environment and engage with digital ecosystems!'* Or something.

Talk of disrupted ecosystems probably goes some way to explaining why the big consulting firms are among the few who seem to be interested in the advertising business. Now we've started to talk a Dunning-Kruger approximation of their language we are fair game.

Just like George Best's dwindling interest in football, the advertising industry seems to have lost interest in our own game. Or we've forgotten why we're in it.

So, where did it all go wrong?

At the close of the 20th century, a powerful idea caught the imagination of the media industry and then the advertising business.

The emerging digital era was to herald the swift death of mass media and mass communications - blunt instruments like TV and newspapers were about to become the forgotten relics of a latter day dark age - as the new technologies ushered in the brave new world of one-to-one communications.

It all seemed pretty plausible.

At the time, none of us even questioned the circular logic of Peppers and Rogers in their 1993 best seller *The One-To-One Future*, as it quickly became the blueprint for the 'new' marketing thinking.

'It is information about individual consumers that will keep a marketer functioning in the 1:1 future. Without individual information, as opposed to market or segment information, 1:1 marketing would not be possible.'

This is 1993, remember. It would be another seven or eight years before the term 'marketing automation' was first uttered, but for the CFO's of the world who saw the money spent on advertising as suspicious at best, a total waste of time at worst, this was the kind of accountability and efficiency story they liked to hear. No more wastage.

Somewhere around this time the seeds were sown that allowed two fundamentally wrong assumptions to become the dominant narratives in advertising and marketing in the digital era.

The first of these is the widespread acceptance and assumption in the industry that 'advertising online' almost exclusively meant 'highly targeted direct response'.

The second is the widespread acceptance and assumption that in order for 'advertising online' to be effective it must always employ the tracking and surveillance of consumers.

Doc Searls said it best, 'Madison Avenue fell asleep, direct response marketing ate its brain, and it woke up as an alien replica of itself.'

When asked, people don't like the idea of being overtly tracked and profiled. In some quarters (the above-mentioned Doc, in particular) there's close to a moral panic over tracking, I'm not sure I subscribe to that view. We're too far in, to go back.

Fundamentally it's what the internet is *for*. Information.

Kevin Kelly suggests that our central choice now is whether the surveillance economy is going to work one-way only, or more of a kind of 'co-veillance'.

'…So that we make tracking and monitoring as symmetrical and transparent as possible. That way the monitoring can be regulated, mistakes appealed and corrected, specific boundaries set and enforced.

A massively surveilled world is not a world I would design (or even desire), but massive surveillance is coming either way because that is the bias of digital technology and we might as well surveil well and civilly.'

Whom we are being tracked by, and to what end, needs sorting.

I agree with Doc that adtech, in its current guise, is full of fraud and malware, incentivises bullshit content over journalism and gives fake news a business model.

But apart from that…

Of course, being followed around the web by ads for stuff they have already bought is annoying. This cheap, clumsy targeting has a knock-on effect in that it may even actually harm those brands that are doing the following.

Implicitly this sends the wrong signal to consumers, especially if an established brand is the signaller.

Signalling theory shows that when we can intuit how much money a company has laid out for an ad campaign, this helps us, unconsciously, make distinctions between brands that have put their money where their mouth is and brands that have not.

Even if - as much of the rhetoric goes - people are demanding and responding to more personalised and relevant 'advertising', why isn't ad-blocking adoption going down?

But from an advertisers point of view, and aside from any ethical considerations, the single biggest failure of adtech is that advertising online to date has simply not been able to deliver on the brand advertising part of the picture.

The internet's spectacular inability to deliver on brand advertising means it is (today) not really a place to be if you want to build a brand, because we have set up the web to only deliver direct response marketing pretending to be advertising in the form of impressions and clicks and an assortment of vanity metrics, coincidentally the easiest things to fake.

We've forgotten the basic idea that brand advertising creates demand and direct response fulfils it. The adtechers and our Silicon Valley robot overlords stepped up, wanted the whole game and we handed it to them on a plate.

The ball has been stolen by the worst kind of *used car salesmen (and their mechanics),* and the actual drivers have had no input.

So where do we go from here?

Psychologists will tell you that humans are pretty good intuitive biologists.

We have innate abilities to be able to identify the kinds of plants that are safe to eat, or animals that are likely to be predators or venomous.

We are also pretty good intuitive psychologists. We can identify what others are thinking and feeling, or what kind of mood they are in with very few cues.

I'd also argue that people are pretty good intuitive media strategists.

We don't know how much a full-page ad in the broadsheet newspaper costs, exactly. But we do know that it was pretty damn expensive.

We don't know exactly how much that retargeting banner ad costs but we know that it's pretty cheap.

Likewise, we can easily and intuitively detect high or low production values that reflect the level of economic investment in any piece of communications. All these indicators are signals.

The kinds of signals that carry an implicit sense of 'cost' on behalf of the signaller can be trusted, to a degree.

Costly signals are reliable. The signaller has put their money where their mouth is.

Researchers Ambler and Hollier quantified this in their consequential study *The Waste in Advertising is the Part that Works*, which we shall return to a few times.

'High perceived advertising expense enhances an advertisement's [persuasiveness] significantly, but largely indirectly, by strengthening perceptions of brand quality.'

Quality online publishers, for example, are beginning to come round to the idea that a viable strategy might be to restrict their premium online inventory, creating scarcity and therefore an opportunity for 'signal' or brand building.

(I worked with a premium fashion title a couple of years ago and this was their exact model. There was no way they were going to sully their web presence with anything other than premium ads and also premium branded content – the same strategy as for the print magazine).

The way an ad is perceived in any vehicle is influenced by both the editorial content, and also on the other ads it shares space with.

So ads in this particular publication were not just sold to anybody who could pay for them.

If anything, the ads were as integral to the experience as the editorial. But what about efficiency? Adtech makes everything more efficient, right?

In so-called Madmen days the media owners took 85 percent of an advertiser's dollar while the agency took the other 15 percent.

The advertiser could then open up the newspaper or switch on the TV and radio and see their ad.

Full transparency? What? This was clearly a broken model!

By way of an amusing aside, I recently had a client who were justifiably alarmed to discover, via a tweet by a vigilant employee, that one of their online ads had appeared on the right-wing news/satire website Breitbart.

The agency was alerted and the ad was removed but the incident opened up a can of brand-safety worms that we could have all done without at the time.

I never mentioned this to the client, but was tempted to say that their ad was:

a) Seen by an actual human being for long enough that they were able to screen grab the page and post it to Twitter.

b) Regardless of whether we agree or disagree with the political sentiment of Breitbart, it is a legitimate news site, written by real journalists - albeit journalists of questionable viewpoint.

This means that the ad in question was already doing somewhat better than 75% of online display.

(The employee herself had been retargeted from somewhere else and followed to Breitbart. Whether she went there deliberately in order to make a point, or this was an indicator of her individual political leanings is not known.)

The quote that follows is pulled from Onora O'Neill's 2002 Reith Lectures series *A Question of Trust.*

Her comments are as apt today as they were then. In the 5th of her lectures, *License to Deceive*, the Cambridge Emeritus Professor of Philosophy was principally referring to the state of journalism but, in 2017, we can apply her insight to what has happened to advertising in general and by advertising technology in particular.

'Do we really gain from heavy-handed forms of accountability? Do we really benefit from...demands for transparency? I am unconvinced.

I think we may undermine professional performance and standards...by excessive regulation, and that we may condone and even encourage deception in our zeal for transparency.'

The final sentence is perhaps the most disturbing.

How can we discern the trustworthy from untrustworthy?

O'Neill argues that we should perhaps focus less on grandiose ideals of transparency and rather more on limiting deception.

O'Neill was some 15 years ahead of my Google/Facebook crunchy-on-the-outside-fluffy-on-the-inside metaphor.

'The new information technologies may be anti-authoritarian, but curiously they are often used in ways that are also anti-democratic. They undermine our capacities to judge others' claims and to place our trust.'

We need to make measurement sexy. It's a topic we need to embrace and give a lot more love to, say the likes of the IAB.

Good luck with that.

Not everything that counts can be counted.

And when trust moves out, measurement moves in.

Full transparency and exposure to skulduggery may even backfire, strengthening the norm that unsavoury behaviours are widespread, and therefore those behaviours are (implicitly) permissible. Or that the behaviour is necessary in order to succeed, a muddling of norms.

We are where we are, and it's going to be a long road back, but the biggest challenge is not that evil criminal masterminds populate agencies - or even some areas of advertising technology - although they do exist. It's more of a cock-up than a conspiracy.

People who, fundamentally, do not understand what advertising is for or how it works ARE increasingly being handed far too much influence in the industry.

In the words of Hanlon's eponymous Razor, 'never attribute to malice that which is adequately explained by stupidity'. But how much can be attributed to stupidity?

The legendary Theodore 'Ted' Sturgeon was, and still is, widely acclaimed as one of the greats in science fiction and horror writing and would have been no stranger to the odd slash of a razor.

He wrote a number of novels, was an early scriptwriter on the promising TV series *Star Trek* in the 50s and 60s and also one of the foremost critics in the sci-fi genre, also penning over 400 reviews before his passing in 1985.

After many years of batting back attacks on the science fiction genre from critics, he had a moment of insight.

This insight became known as Sturgeon's Revelation, later shortened - less dramatically - to Sturgeon's *Law*.

Speaking at the World Science Fiction Convention in Philadelphia in September 1953, Sturgeon responded to 'proper' literary critics who claimed that 'ninety percent of science fiction is crap'.

Ted agreed. Ninety percent of science fiction is indeed crap.

But, he argued, to say ninety percent of science fiction is crap is meaningless, because science fiction conforms to the same trends of quality as all other art forms.

Sturgeon's Law therefore states that ninety percent of everything - all film, literature, products, culture and advertising - is crap.

Less often reported, is Ted's proposed solution to the problem. If we agree that ninety percent of everything is crap, then what's important is to study, learn from and promote the ten percent that isn't crap.

(Maybe 90% is generous, it's more likely closer to 99% but you get the idea.)

In advertising there seems to be a period when any new approach, new platform or technology comes along that - for a time - seems to somehow be viewed as exempt from this law. In the beginning all TV and radio advertising, such was its shiny newness, was likely to be exempt.

Social media marketing, content marketing, QR codes, VR/AR, chatbots, and most recently programmatic delivery and adtech have all arrived, been heralded as the next big thing, then gradually landed in a ditch of disappointment or - as in the case of adtech in its current guise - murky nefariousness.

But if we had remembered Sturgeon's law perhaps we could

have been more critical of practices and theories from the outset and avoided a lot of unpleasantness.

The shortcomings of the majority of adtech have now been fully revealed.

(As another aside, it is peculiar that in this age when information is supposed to disseminate at warp speed mainstream media has only just caught up with what many of us have been discussing for about 4 or 5 years.)

Somehow we have to shift focus and look for the 1%.

Looking for the good.

Where is the good practice? If there is none then how do we create some?

As an industry we've been duped and been cheated, but now we have had our eyes opened.

Will we get fooled again?

Probably, Madison Avenue has often been the road to Abilene.

Anyone who has sat through campaign or brand tracking presentations by supposedly reputable research companies and thought '…am I the only one in this room who thinks this is bullshit?' please raise your hand now.

I thought so. Just about everyone. But we never raised our

hands at the time.

The only way to break out of these cycles is to speak up, ask questions, be sceptical and ask for evidence.

A decent rule of thumb would be to DEMAND that the more extraordinary the claim of any technology platform or gizmo, the stronger the evidence must be to support that claim.

This is not a Luddite rant. Far from it.

Programmatic delivery, automation and advertising technology is inevitable. Very soon all media will be bought and distributed in this way.

Surveillance is also inevitable but if we can work towards balancing symmetry and transparency there's much value to be derived from real behavioural data at this scale. More on that later.

Crappy-ness, however, need not be inevitable.

Not if the programmatic, automation and advertising technology is operated by people who understand how advertising works, what it is for and why we urgently need to figure out and evaluate existing and emerging technologies on their ability or future potential to actually build brands.

The *used car salesmen* and engineers have had their turn, and the results were substantially less than optimal.

Factor in blind-sided publishers, winner-takes-all multinationals being allowed to mark their own homework, the deluge of shitty content, open season for fraudsters and criminals and we've got a big mess to clean up.

At least 90% of the whole internet advertising shooting match was total crap. But its out in the open and we have to move on.

And 90% of everything will always be shit, but it's only a relentless, sceptical, demand for quality and creativity that points the way forward.

The impending death of something or other is reported every other week. The death of this, the death of that, the death of the other and the death of the next thing. The death of advertising in particular.

Mea culpa. About 10 years ago I probably was that douche-bag. As we discussed earlier, I called it my own Dunning-Kruger peak.

But if one is lucky, eventually one gets over one's own bullshit, to a degree.

Or at least goes into recovery.

(I'm taking each day as it comes.)

Perhaps, it all went wrong when we forgot the simple fact that the purpose of advertising is to bring brands, products, services and behaviours to the attention of the people in order that they might buy them or buy into them at the next opportunity.

What if the change the industry *really* needs is to refocus itself towards producing the kind of brilliant, insightful, creative advertising that will get noticed and remembered by consumers. We've more ability to screen out crap than ever before, so should the solution be better ways to do advertising not worse?

If advertising is really dead, can it come back to life?

Back in 1979, the emerging young painter Julian Schnabel presented his two breakthrough solo exhibitions at Mary Boone's gallery in New York.

The shows mainly featured his signature neo-expressionist wax paintings and plate paintings.

Amid the popular and influential art world narrative of the time included widely read articles with titles like 'The End of Painting' and 'Last Exit: Painting' in respected journals such as Artforum.

It should be noted that those essays (penned by critics Douglas Crimp and Thomas Lawson, respectively) should be approached with some caution unless readers are particularly fluent in academic postmodernist mumbo jumbo.

The final nail in painting's coffin had barely been hammered into its place when at the exact same time other commentators began to herald Schnabel's works as 'the RETURN of painting'.

In later years (and looking back), Schnabel - somewhat wryly - reflected:

"I thought that if painting is dead, then it's a nice time to start painting."

It strikes me that there is a real, live emerging opportunity for those advertising agencies that actually want to take advantage of the expanded 21st century media and technology canvas to actually make killer advertising. A crazy idea, but it just might work.

Its worth presenting Schnabel's full remark on the 'return to painting', but looked at through the lens of advertising.

'I thought that if [advertising] is dead, then it's a nice time to start [doing advertising]. People have been talking about the death of [advertising] for so many years that most of those people are dead now.'

Advertising's many detractors are not dead yet, unfortunately. Even more unfortunately a great many are the ones who are supposed to be driving the industry forward, but perhaps their time is coming to an end. Here's hoping.

In later years, and reflecting on his career, George Best famously joked, 'I spent most of my money on booze, birds and fast cars. The rest I just squandered.'

George got it; it's the *waste* that is the part that works.

As for us?

We have neglected imagination, creativity, originality and intelligence – all the fundamentals that make our product occasionally great – and instead, squandered a lot of advertising money on dubious adtech and poor quality direct response that creates no value for publishers, advertisers, consumers and is sending the next generation(s) of real creative talent looking somewhere else, somewhere more *sexy*.

So tell us, George. Where did it all go wrong?

'It had nothing to do with women and booze, car crashes or court cases.

It was purely football.

The great players I'd been brought up with were replaced with players who should not even have been allowed through the door.'

Boom.

What's the story?

Carry on... storytelling!

In a semi-legendary rant the New Yorker-Austrian graphic design giant Stefan Sagmeister splendidly called bullshit on 'storytelling'.

Speaking at a Canadian design festival in 2014, Sagmeister attacked the current vogue in the communications industry for describing what we do as the work of *storytellers*.

'Now everybody's a storyteller,' he says.

'Recently I read an interview with someone who designs roller coasters and he referred to himself as a 'storyteller'. No, [expletive] You are not a storyteller; you're a roller coaster designer! There is this fallacy out there. I don't think I fell for it, but somehow maybe unconsciously I did, you know... I've seen a number of films so I must be able to make a film. People who actually tell stories, meaning people who write novels and make feature films don't see themselves as storytellers. It's all the people who are not storytellers suddenly now want to be storytellers'.

Don't tell him about this book, please.

Although, I'm not sure if Sagmeister expands further on his points in any of the 22 books he has written and published.

Yes, all this is pretty amusing, but is it fair?

Given the prevalence of inane drivel on the internet spouted by communications professionals in the name of brand storytelling it is hard not to side with Stefan.

Where to begin?

In defence of story, let's refer to the early chapters of the splendid *The Storytelling Animal in* which author and literary Darwinist Jonathan Gottschall makes this observation:

'The storytelling mind is allergic to uncertainty, randomness, and coincidence. It is addicted to meaning. If the storytelling mind cannot find meaningful patterns in the world, it will try to impose them. In short, the storytelling mind is a factory that churns out true stories when it can, but will manufacture lies when it can't'.

Why might the mind be wired for storytelling?

'We are an insatiably curious species' says the sociobiologist, EO Wilson '…provided the subjects are our personal selves and people we know or would like to know'

Perhaps we are hard-wired to gossip (albeit within narrow parameters.)

Another evolutionary psychologist and anthropologist

Robin Dunbar agrees, calling gossip 'an instrument of social order and cohesion' - akin to the grooming behaviour common among our cousins in the larger primate world.

Primate grooming is not so much about hygiene, although that is a nice by-product.

Grooming is essentially a substitute for language.

It creates bonds, establishes social status and influences other primates.

Dunbar and other evolutionary psychologists suggest that humans developed language specifically to serve the same social purposes.

(Note: Grooming was simply not practical for early humans. Given their large social groups - around 150 or so - grooming one another would have been an impossible time-suck for our hunter gatherer ancestors.)

Language evolved, as it was a more practical and useful way of keeping up to date with friends and family, and obtaining social information about others in the group.

Particularly information about whom one should trust.

This explains - at least in part - why all of us 21st century humans are still pretty pre-occupied with gossip and stories about other peoples behaviour and reputation.

Reputation became important in this sense because, as a

rule of thumb, it made survival sense to be more generous toward others who were also reputable.

I often afford a wry smile at the call from some corners of the marketing world for 'authentic brand stories'.

This is something of an oxymoron given that it is in the nature of stories to feed our social instincts for gossip by only cherry picking the most dramatic and salient parts in recounting events.

Daniel Nettle, author and Professor of Psychology at Newcastle University echoes EO Wilson:

'Conversations are only interesting to the extent that you know about the individuals involved and your social world is bound into theirs...

Given that dramatic characters are mostly strangers to us, then, the conversation will have to be unusually interesting to hold our attention. That is, the drama has to be an intensified version of the concerns of ordinary conversation.'

He explains that we don't watch films about people going shopping; we watch films about people going shopping who are *having an affair with an ex-lover*.

Similarly, a book about some old geezer who goes fishing is not that interesting.

But a story about an old man who goes fishing off the coast of Cuba and ends up in an epic existential battle with a giant pointy nosed fish while contemplating his own mortality is more compelling.

That's Hemmingway's *Old Man Of The Sea*, of course. A book that is often also used by psychotherapists as a therapeutic aid for hopeless and depressed patients in struggles of 'life against fate'. Get a few copies for your agency library.

To Sagmeister's earlier point, everyone is a storyteller to some degree – inasmuch as this innate allergy to uncertainty, randomness, and coincidence requires it in order that we tell our own story to ourselves.

Among communications professionals perhaps that the ability to create evocative brand stories probably depends on a couple of key skills - not necessarily available to all - and the reason why great creative minds are so valuable.

The first– and this is planner territory for the most part - is the ability to observe and interpret the hidden parts of everyday life (aka insight), then ensure that the drama is an intensified version of these concerns.

Secondly, is the creative's ability to work within our cognitive limitations and make things simple yet still containing enough neuro-juice to get noticed?

(This is not to infer that people are stupid, rather that we have a lot more important things to occupy our minds with than brand stories - simplicity is paramount.)

There's an old maxim that goes along these lines. Any intelligent idiot can take a simple idea and make it complicated. It takes a lot more skill to make the complicated simple.

The great stories - and therefore the great brand stories - always reflect the great universal themes of life and evolutionary study has produced a universal picture of the human mind that can be mapped and reflected in all human activity.

Surviving, finding mates, being a parent, being part of a group and being the hero who triumphs in the face of adversity, for example.

From the ice age to the dole-age there is but one concern.

OK, a few.

Brand storytellers should relax. Perhaps not try so hard.

Storytelling, it seems, is less something that is done to us, and more something we are super skilled in doing to ourselves.

Our innate ability to confabulate and fill in the gaps - often extensive - with plausibility, and preserve some sort of narrative continuity based on the merest scraps of information is nothing short of a marvel.

Interestingly, digital culture is - in a way - a return to a storytelling non-linearity that was core to those human societies in the ages before industrialization, mass production and, in particular, the invention, by Gutenberg, of the printing press.

The idea of a 'Gutenberg Parenthesis' - as arrived at by Prof. L. O. Sauerberg of the University of Southern Denmark and propagated by Thomas Pettitt from the same university - is a way of understanding the period we are emerging from...

'...during which the mediation of texts through time and across space was dominated by powerful permutations of letters, print, pages and books. Our current transitional experience toward a post-print media world dominated by digital technology and the internet can be usefully juxtaposed with that of the period - Shakespeare's - when England was making the transition into the parenthesis from a world of scribal transmission and oral performance...'

In layperson terms, the natural flow of human communication, customs, legends and storytelling was interrupted by the advent of print and, therefore, 'containment', that Pettitt describes as the 'imprisonment' of words.

'They were pressed onto pages, stitched up, bound, with

stories circumscribed by beginning, middle and end -- so unlike story telling and other kinds of cultural production in previous times, when oral traditions meant dynamically changing texts and performances.'

Are we are looking forward and seeing something that looks more like the past than the present? An uncontained, fluid, secondary orality, but digitally-powered and supported by super-literacy? Or is that just more postmodernist horse feathers?

Who knows, but we'll certainly carry on storytelling. Gottschall agrees:

'The way we experience story will evolve, but as storytelling animals, we will no more give it up than start walking on all fours'.

What a waste!

If we could talk to the animals, just imagine it? Chatting to a chimp in chimpanzee!

Lions rely on a couple of principal hunting methods. In the first approach the lion stalks, undercover, getting as close as possible to the target, saving vital energy for a final burst of speed at the end.

Lions can't run very fast over distance.

The second technique involves finding cover - a bush close to a water hole, for example - hiding in it and waiting for unsuspecting dinner to appear.

This second tack is doubly good for the lion, as it can also have a snooze whilst technically 'out hunting'.

A bit like 'working from home'.

Our lion wakes up and sees a young Thomson's gazelle taking a break by the water.

Lion tentatively moves out of the bush, but the alert young gazelle clocks him straight away.

But the gazelle doesn't run.

Nor does he crouch or try to hide.

Instead he turns to face the Lion.

Standing up straight he barks and stamps the ground with his hooves, all the time staring-out his potential attacker.

The lion comes a bit nearer.

Surely the gazelle should get off his mark now?

Nope. He stands his ground, and then begins a series of repeated jumps, using all four legs, a kind of dance known as 'stotting'.

After a number of these jumps he then begins a somewhat leisurely run, shakin' his ass and short black tail at the lion in a kind of gazelle version of 'come and have a go if you think you're hard enough.'

The lion steps back into the bush for another nap.

Why would the gazelle waste time and energy jumping up and down in front of an extremely dangerous predator instead of legging it as fast as it can?

And why does the Lion not go for him?

Biologist Amotz Zahavi asked this same question, and published the findings in 1975 in his hugely influential study *The Handicap Principle*.

Zahavi suggests that the gazelle is 'signalling' to the

predator that it has seen it; and that by 'wasting' time and energy by jumping high in the air rather than running away, it demonstrates in a reliable way that it is capable of outrunning the Lion.

'Even parties in the most adversarial relationships, such as prey and predator, may communicate, provided that they have a common interest: in this case, both want to avoid a pointless chase.'

The gazelle is communicating - implicitly - to the Lion as if to say:

'Look at the amount of energy I can expend, and still get away from you. Let's not waste each other's time. Go and find something to eat that you might have a chance of catching.'

In a nutshell *The Handicap Principal* describes how - in order to be effective - signals must be:

1. Reliable

2. And in order to be reliable, signals have to be costly.

It's an elegant idea: waste makes sense.
'Conspicuous' waste in particular.

'By wasting [conspicuously], one proves conclusively that one has enough assets to waste and more. The investment - the waste itself - is just what makes the advertisement reliable.'

Returning to researchers Tim Ambler and E. Ann Hollier in *The Waste in Advertising Is the Part That Works*, they wondered if the same thing applied in brand advertising.

The pair devised a number of signalling tests including showing 'expensive-looking' and 'degraded' versions of the same TV commercials to experimental subjects, and found that the perceived expense was influential in reported perceptions of brand quality.

'The perceived extravagance of an advertisement contributes to advertising effectiveness by increasing credibility. It draws especially on the *Handicap Principle* in biology: animals use wasteful characteristics to signal their exceptional biological fitness. It hypothesises that excesses in advertising work in a similar way by signalling brand fitness…high perceived advertising expense enhances an advertisement's [persuasiveness] significantly, but largely indirectly, by strengthening perceptions of brand quality'

The most important fact about a signal is that both senders and receivers benefit from its use.

At the core of signalling is the idea that businesses are constantly communicating through their actions, even when they are not intentionally communicating.

Over time, we implicitly learn that heavily advertised brands are of a high quality, and because advertising causes salience of the brand name, most times we can infer high quality from recognition alone.

It is the increasing *absence of such signal* that is becoming one of the core problems we have with digital advertising today, and one we urgently need to solve.

Faris has spoken of it in terms of a *Malthusian trap.*

'Every time some new space opens up in culture, we rush to fill it, create an arms race and destroy the space.'

It's a rat trap Judy, and we've been caught.

There was a *proper* rat problem in the sewers of the Vietnamese capital, Hanoi, back during the first period of French colonial rule in the early 1900's.

Bob Geldof wasn't around so in order to combat the rat problem - and resulting nasties like bubonic plague - the French authorities swiftly acted to rid their new sewers of vermin with an incentive for the Hanoi citizens.

For every dead rat tail delivered to the appointed rat repository, the good citizen would receive a cash reward.

Behavioural economics had not been invented yet and the French officials had no Nudge Unit on hand to advise on the potential pitfalls of this strategy.

Quelle surprise, it was not long until the entrepreneurial Vietnamese farmers began specifically breeding their own rat colonies for the exact purpose of cashing in.

When the French authorities realized that the crafty locals had been gaming the incentive they immediately cancelled the scheme.

As the bottom had now fallen out of the rat-farming market, all remaining farmed rats were released and the problem became three or four times worse than it had been in the beginning.

Fast forward to 1997 and Wells Fargo Bank's CEO Dick Kovacevich launches a 'cross-selling' initiative called 'Going for Gr-Eight'.

The idea was that customers could be persuaded to buy eight financial products from the bank and eight rhymes with great (geddit?). Kovacevich's objective - getting customers to buy as many products as possible - was not unreasonable. But how many products was a reasonable goal?

In the end, eight turned out to not be the magic number and on September 8, 2016, Wells Fargo was ordered to pay a combined $185 million in penalties after being found responsible for incentivising 'fraudulent conduct . . . on a massive scale'. The bank's internal audit found that between 2011 and 2015 employees had opened more than 1.5 million deposit accounts and more than 500,000 credit-card accounts on behalf of customers that were, most likely, unauthorised.

And then by August 2017 Wells Fargo announced it had uncovered a further 70 percent more potentially bogus accounts. Over 5,000 employees were ultimately fired for opening these fake accounts in order to meet the aggressive sales quotas dictated by '…gr-eight'.

The bank blamed the fraud on the incentives. In this case 'employees trying to hit minimum goals to *keep their jobs*'.

The bank's average product per customer was about three. Ironically, this was slightly on the high end of what was typical - inbetween 2 to 3 products per customer was the category norm. Wells Fargo customers typically held about 3 because of the size of the brand. That they even assumed most consumers would own eight or more financial products in total is strange.

It should be said that all this unpleasantness could have easily been avoided if the bank had a basic understanding of loyalty metrics and Ehrenberg's Double Jeopardy law.

Loyalty measures for brands are usually similar for brands in a category, and follow the Double Jeopardy Law. Smaller brands are smaller because they have fewer customers who are slightly less loyal. Improving loyalty is possible, but it always comes from penetration.

So much for incentives. Or, more accurately, if the only way to achieve the goals required to unlock the incentives is cheating then people will cheat.

In the beginning, adtech was simply a handy means for publishers to get shot of remnant inventory in a bargain bin - and make an easy buck - and a automated process to save time for the media buyer.

The promise of ultra-efficient, simplified, one-stop buying of multi-screen inventory was pretty appealing. The promise of knowing where every single dollar was spent, and whether it 'performed' even more so.

But none of that ever materialised.

Because, as we plugged more and more media into this same platform it started to become a problem.

Economics is all about incentives, and this system had created huge incentives for nefarious third parties to try and exploit it.

Pretty soon aspiring media 'moguls' cottoned on to the fact that all they had to do to make a load of money was create an 'audience' for their 'content' and the programmatic systems would buy it.

The algorithms don't care what is real traffic or bot traffic, neither are they designed to distinguish between original quality content and scraped or cut-n-paste pages.

Just like the French colonials back in Hanoi and Wells

Fargo's cross-sell debacle, we've created a rat tail marketplace, in which - at best - the unscrupulous sellers have all the information and use it to take unfair advantage of ignorant buyers.

So armed with some moody malware, almost anyone can make a bot-net army and create a massive 'audience' very easily. Or even go 'legit', and buy the audience.

It's adland's own game of whack-a-mole, once a fix is found to combat one type of online ad fraud, a new one pops up and each new type of fraud becomes more sophisticated and adaptive as we try to prevent it. Fun and games.

But, at some point very soon we are going to have to seriously figure out how the hell to build brands on the internet, or if we even can.

Saving the world

Can brands really be altruistic?

Different philosophers define altruism in different ways, however most definitions will generally play in and around describing altruistic behaviours as actions that benefit others rather than oneself.

The term altruism (French, *altruisme*) was coined by the 19th century philosopher - incidentally, also the founder of the discipline we now know as sociology (although we won't hold that against him) - Auguste Comte.

He described altruism as our 'moral *obligation* to renounce self-interest and live for others'

Aside from ethics, altruism in biology similarly describes a range of behaviours that may be performed by animals, which benefit others while seemingly to their own disadvantage.

We say 'seemingly' as there is no moral lens that can be applied.

For instance, by behaving altruistically, an organism may reduce it's own chances of survival, or the number of offspring it is likely to produce itself, but give a boost to the likelihood that other organisms that share its genes may survive and produce offspring.

It doesn't make any Darwinian sense to share food with just anybody, it is far more sensible to share with your relatives - they are genetically similar to you.

The costs and benefits of animal altruism in the biological sphere are measured in terms of the resulting reproductive fitness, or expected number of genetic descendants.

It is therefore reasonable to suggest that the biological notion of altruism is somewhat different to the ethical concept.

For humans, an act would only be called 'altruistic' if it was done with the conscious moral intention of helping another, but in the biological sense there is no such requirement.

So, which definition is appropriate when talking about *brand altruism*?

In 1973 the Russian biologist Theodosius Dobzhansky famously wrote 'Nothing in Biology Makes Sense Except in the Light of Evolution'.

It could also be noted that nothing in brand behaviour makes sense except in the light of evolution.

Brands, like organisms, have two principle concerns. Survival and reproduction.

Survival should be a self-evident notion, just staying in business. For reproduction we could think about the number of category entry points in which the brand is salient and perhaps breadth of distribution as measures of fitness.

But, so-called, brand altruism, is perhaps better understood through the lens of *Biological Market Theory.*

Animals (including humans) can be observed exchanging benefits through reciprocity mechanisms. This happens in a variety of ways and in a variety of scenarios, however the common thread is that benefits in kind almost always find their way back to the original giver.

This (r)evolutionary theory of reciprocal altruism was originally developed and published in 1971 by the biologist Bob Trivers in order to explain to explain instances of (apparent) altruism among unrelated organisms, including members of different species.

Trivers' basic idea was pretty straightforward: it may payback to help another, if there is an expectation of the favour being returned in the future.

Equivalent to the heuristic 'You scratch my back, I'll scratch yours'. The classic tit-for-tat strategy.

The cost of helping is offset by the likelihood of the return benefit, allowing the behaviour to evolve by natural selection.

However, even reciprocal altruists are vulnerable to exploitation by rogue non-altruists.

Suppose we have a group or category - let's say supermarkets - made up exclusively of altruists, all playing nicely together, and placing the benefit of their suppliers and customers above their own needs.

It only takes a single mutant to enter the category, adopt some selfish policies to gain relative fitness advantages then the altruistic system starts to collapse and eventually become overtaken.

Altruism, by definition, incurs a fitness cost.

So why would a brand perform a costly act?

As an aside, it's probably no accident that the current popularity of the brand altruism idea corresponds with the development on another on the consumer side - virtue signalling.

Much has been written elsewhere on the pros and cons of online virtue signalling - the highly conspicuous expression of particular moral values done primarily with the intention of gaining status within a social group - but suffice to say that (and depending on which report one believes) apparently upwards of 70% of millennials will claim that the social responsibility record and 'altruism' of a brand is a major factor in their propensity to buy or use that brand. Sure.

It is also claimed by many that this generation of consumers are even willing to PAY MORE for altruistic brands! Right.

Maybe so, but what cannot be disputed is the propensity the connected generation to perform actions (mostly online) that signal to others that 'I'm a good person'. It's worth noting that the message need not be actually accompanied by actually doing anything good. This opens the window for brand altruism as a virtue-outsourcing vehicle.

The 'feelings' of self-righteousness are so good so it's no wonder that we are inclined to seek them - and will happily take a shortcut to acquire them.

So is brand altruism something of a misnomer, and simply a contemporary biological market tactic pandering to the current cultural mode for a particular flavour of virtue signalling?

If this were the case then that may cause some significant cognitive dissonance for the authenticity seeking future consumers.

(Not all is lost however. Lack of *millennial* buying power notwithstanding, there is still much fun to be had given that the only thing people seem to like more than virtue signalling is judging other people!)

Perhaps another idea to consider is this. Brand altruism may simply be interpreted as signal. A costly and strategic signal, that provides an honest indicator of quality.

A brand might make a strategic investment in altruism that acts simply as a signal of its ability to BE altruistic - the brand signals that it has the assets to do so.

In this sense, brand altruism is simply another form of costly signalling the same as investing in high quality advertising and equivalent to the 'handicap' for which the peacock's tail has become a metaphor.

It's kinda altruism, but it's competitive.

Let's return to Ambler and Hollier's *The Waste in Advertising,* again.

'The perceived extravagance of [a brand's altruistic acts] contributes to advertising effectiveness by increasing credibility. It draws especially on the Handicap Principle in biology: animals use wasteful characteristics to signal their exceptional biological fitness. It hypothesizes that excesses in [altruism] work in a similar way by signalling brand fitness...'

In summary, we should probably understand this emerging idea of brand altruism as a part of the brand marketing process through which brands compete with each other in terms of conspicuous generosity (or if you prefer, observable competitive altruism) in order to enhance the status, reputation and perceived quality of the brand.

If some good is worth doing, it's worth doing in public. And, of course, the more salient the 'altruistic' acts of the brand are then the associated 'generosity' traits transfer to buyers and users of the brand, more grist to our virtue signalling.

For sure, it is good that brands may wish to contribute to a greater good, or to society as a whole.

But let's not get too caught up with esoteric notions of 'pure' altruism.

Rest easy advertisers and marketers. We can make the world better and still be our selfish, insecure and status-seeking selves.

Or just believe in magic.

Never trust a hippy

Do you believe in magic?

There's a clip in an episode of illusionist Derren Brown's TV show in which he predicts he can flip a coin 10 times in a row and it will come up heads every time.

He proceeds to do exactly this, flipping the coin into a bowl 10 times and it comes up heads every time, just as predicted.

Magic, right? Or at least some sort of quantum entanglement?

The truth is less mysterious; he flipped the coin for about ten hours straight until he produced the sequence he wanted. His team then edited out all the 'wrong' flips and broadcast only the successful sequence.

Similarly, you'll be familiar with the famous thought experiment that describes how an infinite number of monkeys bashing on typewriters for long enough, will result in one of them eventually writing a novel. But what are the chances our monkey author would bash out a follow-up, or another monkey would come up with anything?

Will there ever be a follow up to this NYT bestseller you

are reading (and who owns the film rights)?

Is there any evidence that featuring cats in your video makes it more likely that it will be successful?

Perhaps the success of some cat videos is simply proportionate to the huge number of cat videos that are out there in the first place, the vast majority of which receive little or no views at all, bar their proud owners.

In the coin-flipping skit, monkeys who produce nothing, and the mountain of unwatched cat videos that are forgotten, we only see the survivors.

Survivorship bias is the error of looking only at features that winners appear to have in common, and assuming they're the only reasons why things are successful.

If, instead of being a 21st century advertising douchebag, you had been a member of a US bomber crew in WW2 your chances actually making it back from any given mission, were on the side of slim.

The nature of the work meant that bombers were out for a long time, they were massive cumbersome planes visible from a long way away, and their ability to do serious damage if successful meant they were the number one targets of both the guns on the ground and in the air.

For the bomber crews, each subsequent mission piled up

the odds against them making it back the next time.

And the factories couldn't make new planes quick enough to replace the ones that went down.

The situation was unsustainable.

In the hope of a solution the military engineers examined the bombers that made it back from their missions.

Patterns started to emerge. They saw the damage tended to accumulate in the same places.

They observed clusters of bullet holes along both wings, down the centre of the bomber's body and around the tail gunner area.

The answer was clear. The bombers needed more armour.

However they couldn't just reinforce the entire plane, the weight would prevent them from even taking off.

So, based on the data they had, the obvious solution was to put thicker protection where they see the most damage, and ramp up reinforcement in the areas where the bullet holes clustered.

Just to be absolutely sure they were doing the right thing, the engineers called in a statistician, one Abraham Wald.

Wald was a member of the military's 'Applied Mathematics Panel' - a secret boffin unit working out of Columbia

University applying the science of probability and statistics to the war effort.

And it's a jolly good job they did, as Wald saw immediately that they were about to make exactly the wrong decision.

Because the common patterns of bullet holes actually showed where the planes were strongest.

The holes showed where a bomber could be hit repeatedly and still make it back.

The planes that didn't make it home were being hit in different places.

Until Wald's intervention the military were overly focused on the planes that made it home and almost made a potentially catastrophic decision by ignoring the planes that got shot down.

Management guru Tom Peters studied several successful companies (enjoying) and published a book - *In Search of Excellence* - outlining what he saw as a 'success formula' based on those things that the companies appeared to have in common. There was nothing much wrong with Peters' eight (gr-eight?) 'themes' – *bias for action, stick to your knitting, productivity through people* are a few. It's just that many of the organisations highlighted by Peters then found themselves having difficulties within a few years, while employing virtually the same strategies that had made them successful.

Just like our Air Force engineers, it's easy for marketers and agencies to get distracted by these 'excellence' case studies or by so-called 'purpose-driven' brands.

Because the graveyard is littered with failed brands with the same purposeful ideologies.

Or, on a more mundane level, marketers are distracted the high response rates and dramatic ROI that appears to fall out of highly targeted direct response. On the surface it appears logical.

But these sales often come from people who are most likely to buy, anyway. The cluster of bullet holes that registered on the wings of the planes that made it home.

And the bigger the plane the bigger those clusters will naturally be. This is because the bigger brands in any given category tend to have slightly higher rates of bullet hole frequency (and loyalty) than their smaller competitors.

For just about any brand, attracting the mass of category buyers who are light and non-buyers of the particular brand - just like the bullet holes that didn't show up, or barely registered on the bombers that made it home - holds the key as to whether the mission is going to be successful or not.

One does not have to look far on the internet to find studies that appear to show how a single factor, such as company culture, customer focus or a company's commitment to social responsibility, lead to high performance.

It could just as easily be argued that its precisely because companies are high performing that they subsequently benefit from better culture, or are able to contribute to social responsibility activities.

More recently Richard Shotton and Aiden O'Callaghan published a splendid report debunking the idea that brand 'purpose' is a driver of success as popularized Peters and, more recently, by Jim Stengel in the bestselling business book *Grow*.

It turns out that spectacularly failing brands like Nokia and Kodak were just as ideal-driven as the successful brands Stengel chose to feature.

But those examples didn't fit the story.

And we prefer the story, if we are honest.

Even half of the firms that featured in Naomi Klein's savage 'indictment' of western capitalism *'No Logo'* have now gone belly up. Not even post-modernists are safe from these biases.

As Gottschall told us in an earlier chapter:

'The storytelling mind is a factory that churns out true stories when it can, but will manufacture lies when it can't.'

In a classic piece of corporate 'purpose' myth-making *Ice Cream Social: The Struggle for the Soul of Ben & Jerry's* - penned by the hired gun journo Brad Edmondson – we are informed that the consumers who buy Ben & Jerry's ice cream are all intensely devoted to the brand's social purpose, and it is this single factor explains the success of the company!

And what's more, the company's hippy roots and support for left-leaning social issues, like the occupy movement back in the day, meant that they did not sell even ice cream to conservatives.

B&J's buyers are exclusively affluent, middle-aged, urban liberals, and intensely devoted.

When I queried this point to the author on Twitter, pointing out that Ben and Jerry's sales patterns will, in all likelihood, conform to the same patterns as any other FMCG brand - i.e. the vast majority of it's sales over a year will come from light buyers who buy the product only once or twice in that period - he responded with the following:

'B&J's success comes from connecting to a passionate segment. The vast majority are not their concern.'

Now, as a piece of brand marketing collateral a bit of myth-building is never a bad thing, so fair play on that one. The small group of employees and even smaller group of B&J fanatics who believe in this are probably the market for the book.

The B&J story is, of course, classic counter-culture to sell-out journey of cognitive dissonance.

The short version. In 1978 Ben and Jerry, a couple of slightly out of date diet-hippies have an ahead-of-their-time-idea and set up an 'artisanal' ice cream shop in a former gas station in Burlington, Vermont.

The ice cream parlour gets popular locally, largely due to the quirky distinctiveness of our two protagonists, and a quirky distinctive product.

Before you know it they are beginning to establish a distribution network among grocery stores and supermarkets.

This draws the attention of media and marketing commentators, some national media coverage hails their product as the best of it's kind in the country, all of which leads to more distribution and more rapid growth.

However now, our heroes are faced with a sell-out conundrum. Quite quickly this thing has turned into a pretty viable business drawing lots of interest from 'the man' in various guises, and the lure of national distribution and even bigger profits.

Because, as the furry freak brothers are now starting to realise, this is the engine of capitalism and they are deep in the belly of the beast (albeit in bellbottoms).

Every new anti-establishment approach business or thing

that starts off as some sort of alternative to the mainstream - more artisanal, authentic or rebellious - eventually gets acquired or incorporated by the establishment and resold back (often completely intact) to the mass market looking for things to consume that *signal* their alternative status to others.

Potter and Heath neatly captured this in *The Rebel Sell.* Any act of attempting to run counter to the culture is what creates the next wave of culture that the next wave of counter-culture will want to counter.

Indeed, 'the man' does come calling, chequebook in hand. B&J ink a deal in 1986 for distribution by Dreyers (a Nestle company), within two years they have also a national chain of 'scoop shops' and are picking up Businessmen of the Year accolades from none other than, that other old counter-culture hippy, Ronald Reagan.

Shortly before signing with Dreyers, swift hippy realignment is established, as the company sets up a foundation and directs a portion of pre-tax profits each year into grants which 'grass-roots' community projects can apply for.

As the 80's turn into the 90's the tide is turning, B&Js is in decline and not profitable. It seems that the hippy ethical business success might be a bit of a blip. Something has to change.

It seems that in the cold light of day, far from being the main driver of growth, the company's social mission was a luxury it could no longer afford.

B&J's is still a $200 million dollar business, but reality bites, the firm is unprofitable so a new shareholder value and growth specialist CEO is appointed, and he engineers the sale to Unilever.

The counter-culture to corporate sell-out cycle is complete. And the company is now faced with a big *cognitive dissonance conundrum.*

This little hippy company that set out it's stall against the mainstream has got bigger and bigger and become the mainstream. Not only that, it's new master is Unilever the world's third-largest consumer goods company, subject to the ire of the likes of Greenpeace on the issues of deforestation and unsustainable palm oil while also allegedly responsible for up to 4% of global green house gas emissions.

Death or glory becomes just another story.

With Unilever as your new boss, what's a hippy to do?

Like cult leaders who predict the end of the world then backtrack when it doesn't happen, Brad resolves his own *cognitive dissonance* easily.

'Why does Unilever, the second-largest food company in

the world, allow one of its wholly owned subsidiaries to embrace radical street protestors and take other positions that it knows will piss off millions of potential buyers of Unilever products?'

The simple answer is that Unilever knows very well that the hundreds of millions of buyers of Unilever brands have no idea that they are buying Unilever brands, are not even vaguely interested in whether they are Unilever brands or not, and the embracing of radical street protests or whatever of Ben and Jerry's is of little or no interest to the vast majority of the buyers of that particular brand. They just want some ice cream.

Because Unilever knows that the so-called counter-culture is actually the engine of capitalism.

For Unilever to continually find new companies to buy, and therefore continue to oil the machine, these companies have to come from somewhere.
But no...

'Again, it goes back to the independent board. Ben Cohen and Jerry Greenfield did not want to sell their company in 2000. They agreed to do it only after Unilever signed a contract that created the board, which exists in perpetuity.'

Presumably the three hundred million dollars was also a factor.

'In addition to protecting product quality, this board also has the legal power to ensure that the company's investment in edgy political causes continues, and that their spending on social mission activities grows with Ben & Jerry's sales.'

Well, we all love to believe a good story.

As the philosopher George Costanza once told a different Jerry, 'Just remember, it's not a lie if *you* believe it'.

For Ben and Jerry's idealist hippy roots the dream is never over.

The tale of the global brand that grew by staying true to its values, never really selling-out and connecting emotionally to only it's intensely devoted loyal fans makes for a great feelgood story inside the company to resolve the inevitable inner conflict that comes with any sell-out.

And it's fantastic that Ben and Jerry's do these things for their local community, at a grass-roots level.

I'm sure we all applaud.

But none of these things have anything to do with why they are one of the most recognisable brands in the supermarket freezer section.

For a brand that has 40% of the US luxury ice cream market to be sustained by the small group of devoted ultra loyal superfans would mean that these fans would likely to be somewhat on the overweight side given the amount of product they would need to consume.

This is not, in any way, how brands get built.

The real story of the success of Ben and Jerry's is somewhat more straightforward and explainable by universal laws of marketing.

Ben and Jerry's, over time has become a highly distinctive brand, easily noticed and remembered, with great distribution that's easy to buy for lots of different types of people.

Yes, they have some very loyal buyers. And some Nazis, too. But not proportionately any more than any other brand. It's the same for everyone.

And in the ice cream category heavy buyers will be literally heavy buyers as the probably consume an equal amount of Haagen-Dazs too.

Edmondson's story might make an entertaining book, but at its root it's fiction.

Most of Ben and Jerry's customers only buy the brand very infrequently. But there are millions of these buyers.

This is how they got big. And for the vast majority of these customers Ben and Jerry's social mission is of no interest whatsoever and has no impact whatsoever on their purchasing behaviour. Myself included. I like the Cherry Garcia, although I've never made it through an entire Grateful Dead album.

'It's much harder to run a mission-driven company than it is to run one that is simply devoted to making a profit', says Edmondson. What has he been smoking?

I tried to get him on the phone but he was out for a mud bath with Simon Sinek.

Swing when you're winning

Or, mistaking outcomes for inputs.

Is it that successful strategy is really just a process of skilfully interacting with chance?

It could be that successful strategy emerges simply because some people are better at interacting with chance and bad strategy comes from the failure to take chance opportunities by confusing outcomes with inputs and being too easily distracted by halo effects.

And, as we've observed, it turns out that many of the things that we commonly believe to be *contributions* to company performance are in fact *attributions*.

Skill is a factor, but so is luck. Skill allows you to make punts that are a bit more informed, but it's no guarantee of success. Success is, for the most part, the result of decisions made under conditions of uncertainty, and always shaped in part by factors outside our control.

As Daniel Kahneman famously explained, 'A stupid decision that works out well becomes a brilliant decision in hindsight.'

Who can forget the story of Dick Rowe, the infamous head of A&R at Decca Records in the 1960s?

He was the 'idiot' who turned down the Beatles, and claimed that 'guitar music is on the way out in the 60s.'

How could this clanger have conspired?

On a freezing new year's day 1962 the nascent Beatles had driven the 200 miles to London from Liverpool, arriving just 15mins before their 11am booking at Decca's studio, and then recorded a 15 song demo in just under an hour. The set consisted mainly of covers (the Hamburg stuff from their eclectic live repertoire). The tapes have been released in recent years and, to be fair, the session didn't reflect the Fabs in top form.

But poor Dick Rowe wasn't even present at the recording and asked his junior Decca A&R guy, Mike Smith (who had recorded the session) to make the call between the Fabs and another beat combo auditioning the same day, the Tremeloes.

The Tremeloes got the gig, possibly influenced by the fact that the boys came from Dagenham (Smith figured it would be easier to work with a risky new investment based in East London than one based in Liverpool).

Rowe's 'guitar music is on the way out' quote was one of several knock-backs given to the persistent Fabs manager Brian Epstein who wouldn't take no for an answer from

Smith, and so continued to pester Rowe throughout the early months of '62. Less widely known is that The Beatles fateful Decca session tapes also got them turned down by a number of other labels including Columbia, HMV, Pye and Philips.

Despite his legacy, Rowe was no mug. He recognised and signed a host of artists that defined the 60s beat-boom including Them (featuring the young Van Morrison), the Moody Blues, the Zombies, John Mayall's Bluesbreakers (the band that launched Eric Clapton), Tom Jones and the Small Faces. And following a tip, from George Harrison no less, in 1963 signed up a promising blues influenced combo rocking out in west London called the Rolling Stones.

'Business is full of mysteries, but none greater than this: what really works?' So asks business theorist Phil Rosenzweig who unpacked much of the flawed logic prevalent in contemporary business thinking, in _The Halo Effect_.

In finding out what works, Rosenzweig advises that we should be mindful of dazzling halo effects from apparent winners, and examine the failures a bit more closely. And, as in the Dick Rowe example, vice versa.

Firstly, all strategies involve managing risk and uncertainty.

Execution is also uncertain. What works well for one situation may not be effective for another, however similar.

As we've just explored, randomness plays a greater role in

success (and failure) than we like to admit and bad outcomes don't always mean that mistakes were made.

(Likewise, successful outcomes don't necessarily mean that we made brilliant decisions.)

'Frankie me boy you don't know,
You have the perfect voice to sing calypso'

Long before Beatlemania, The pop stars of big-band years, the period from the mid-30's to mid 40's and often described as the 'swing era', were the band leaders.

These were usually virtuoso instrumentalists and 'conductors' of sorts.

The likes of Louis Armstrong, Count Basie and Tommy Dorsey are among some of the most well known.

For the most part the singers in the big bands had to make do with being of secondary importance to the band leaders.

For example, the Tommy Dorsey Orchestra's vocal chores were handled some semi-anonymous young fella by the name of Frank Sinatra.

The natural order of things was disrupted, however, in part due to a somewhat random event.

A strike in 1942 by the US musicians' union, in a dispute over royalty payments led to a temporary stop on any new recordings being made, as union musicians halted recording for any record company.

Live performances were still permitted, but this posed problems for both the radio stations (who had only just got their heads around playing records in the first place) and, of course, the record companies themselves.

Among the workarounds that the radio DJs employed were, importing new records from outside the US and staging a wholesale revival of pre-40s recordings.

Things were not so simple for the record companies, however.

For a start, early developments in the emerging and popular new jazz style known later as bebop - being honed by the likes of Charlie Parker and Dizzy Gillespie - were never properly recorded (the Gutenberg parenthesis again).

We can still lament this today.

Around the same time as the strike Frank Sinatra was becoming one of the first vocalists to emerge in his own right and had signed a solo deal with Columbia Records. Columbia wanted to get Sinatra product out as fast as possible. In order to get around the no-musicians rule, Sinatra suggested that they hire master arranger Alec Wilder and vocal group the Bobby Tucker Singers as back up.

Very soon the rest of the industry cottoned on to the fact

that the musicians strike didn't apply to the singers in the band. The MU only represented players of actual instruments so the labels quickly put together vocal only groups featuring the big band back up singers - mimicking instrumental arrangements 'acapella' - and featuring the main vocalists pushed up front.

Not only was a new genre born but also by the time the strike ended the market itself had moved on and a host of other vocalists who previously had to stand in the shadow of the band leaders were following Frank's lead and becoming the new stars. While this flip would have probably happened anyway it's not much of a stretch to speculate that the situation perhaps brought the singers' day forward, somewhat.

It's best described as a synchronicity - a 'meaningful' coincidence. A sequence of events that cannot be fully explained by simple cause and effect but are still connected.

And set the tone for all manner of Elvis-ness and James Brown-ness to come down the line.

The story of how the record industry and others were slow to recognise how digital distribution etc would impact their business model, and the consequences that followed, are well documented.

But, frankly, this was not always the way.

Welcome to our hole

Get a grip on yourself.

If some band of galaxy-wandering aliens should stumble upon this planet earth, or even if they are already here, our species has but one thing worthy of their attention and study.

And it's not our science or technology, as one might immediately imagine.

Yes, we're the only species to have achieved civilization on this planet - so far - but we would have nothing to teach our interplanetary explorers about technology.

The mere presence of these extraterrestrial visitors proves that our technology must be vastly inferior to theirs. Or else it would be us visiting them.

So what could aliens learn from us humans that would have any value to them?

The biologist E.O. Wilson posed the above questions in his mighty tome *The Meaning Of Human Existence.*

Professor Wilson is Emeritus in Entomology for the Department of Organismic and Evolutionary Biology at

Harvard University - amongst other chairs - the world's leading expert on ants and generally regarded as the 'godfather' of sociobiology (a close cousin of evolutionary psychology).

The Meaning Of Human Existence is some fairly light bedtime reading, as you would infer from its whimsical title.

In it Wilson argues that the only thing humans have that would interest the little green men is the 'humanities'.

By 'humanities' we're not including the assorted flavours of postmodernist gobbledygook that have infected universities in recent times, and are unfortunately beginning to spread into other institutions. We're simply referring to our history, philosophy and politics. Our languages, literature and other creative arts like drama, painting and music. Our design, architecture, our media, communications and other cultural products - strapping on our guitars and playing rock'n'roll.

Human creativity.

These products of human popular culture are to modern day anthropologists and psychologists what fossils and bones represent to palaeontologists. Although human minds do not fossilise, these cultural products, created by our minds, do.

Even so, most scientists would agree that the total sum of everything that humans know about proper science is less than five hundred years old and perhaps our major technological achievement to date - the internet - has only existed for around 20 years. So, even though this progress is pretty spectacular it's safe to say that we're still in the very early days of science on this planet.

'Theoretical physics consists of a small number of laws and a great many accidents', according to particle physicist Murray Gell-Mann.

As a humble planner, and one who subscribes wholeheartedly to the evidence-based approach, of course I lean on science heavily to shape the development of strategy and would suggest that the very best work done in advertising has also always been based on a small number of laws and a great many accidents.

And the cultural fossils of advertising have been, and always will be, the creative ideas and executions. If this all sounds misty-eyed for parts of advertising's past, maybe it is.

Many of the cultural fossils produced by the likes of, say, Gossage, Bernbach and even Ogilvy in the 50s and 60s, stand head and shoulders above a lot of what passes for branded communications today. We still remember them, for a start.

That may sound *argumentum ad antiquitatem* to some; I'd remind them that many of Gossage's ideas took 40 years to permeate the mainstream.

The opposite is, naturally, *argumentum ad novitatem.* Routinely and repeatedly overestimating the new and modern, prematurely and without investigation.

For instance, each year we are traditionally dumped upon from the *Dunning-Krugerati* with predictions around which 'game-changing revolutions' we should expect in the next 12 months.

Less headline-worthy but more accurate would be to predict that next year will be very similar to this one, with the only changes being so small you'll barely notice.

Having said that, if any little green men have landed and are lurking around the air-con vents inside your agency then one doubts they would have been particularly impressed with how we've been handling the business of brand building on this planet of late.

In particular our misguided obsession with our primitive technology (for it's own sake), over ideas.

It's a long, long way from idea-rich 'For Mash Get Smash' (I'm guessing they would like that one) to the idea-void of tracking pixels, ad fraud and indiscriminate fetishisation of any and all 'data' (hey, *data* sounds much more sexy than *information*).

No doubt any intergalactic visitors would chuckle at our marketing automation systems in a similar way that those Smash *celetoid* alien robots did at our rudimentary potato mashers.

The rise and imminent fall of the current version of adtech that we've already lamented, is directly connected to the prevalent false belief that communications will succeed through technology alone.

This has never been and will never be the case.

If it's ever going to work it will be through *autonomation*. Automation with a human touch.

I'm reminded of this bold statement from former four-term Louisiana Governor Edwin Edwards made in his address to the Montreal Enlightenment Conference.

He could just as easily be talking about our Silicon Valley robot overlords.

"Without the humanities [sic] to teach us how history has succeeded or failed in directing the fruits of technology and science to the betterment of our tribe of homo sapiens, without the humanities to teach us how to frame the discussion and to properly debate the uses-and the costs-of technology, without the humanities to teach us how to safely debate how to create a more just society with our fellow man and woman, technology and science would eventually default to the ownership of-and misuse by-the most influential, most powerful, most feared among us."

The ongoing search to unravel the human condition will continue to rely on uncovering and analyzing the products of human creativity. In the advertising business, this is the stuff that we produce and these are the cultural fossils that we will leave for future generations, and perhaps visiting aliens, to discover.

Whilst the outputs of our science and technology might not tickle their tentacles, our scientific method would be interesting, given the scope it affords for creativity.

There's a Bill Bernbach quote that appears from time to time. It's the one where Bill takes aim at a particular flavour of advertising that was popular in the early 60's.

'There are a lot great technicians in advertising. And unfortunately they talk the best game. They can give you fact after fact after fact. They are the scientists of advertising. But there's one little rub. Advertising is fundamentally persuasion and persuasion happens to be not a science, but an art.'

When Bernbach goes after 'science', I'd propose that he is really just offering the 'creativity' counter position to the harder selling advertising as championed by the likes of his rival, Rosser Reeves.

Reeves was influenced by the writings of Claude Hopkin who had published a 'manual' for this kind of functional approach entitled *Scientific Advertising* and was dismissive of overly creative executions.

Over time Bill's statement has become contentious, and fuels the continuous Art v Science false dichotomy.

As with most dichotomies the truth is more about the entwinement of the two propositions. I'd argue that when Bill says 'science' he really means 'formulaic'. I'd also argue that Bill himself might have been more scientific in his approach than the 'scientists' that he found irritating.

The Scientific Method is an organised way that helps scientists, strategists or creatives answer a question or begin to solve a problem. There are five basic principles.

1. Start with an observation.

If you're not naturally curious about the world then you are unlikely to be able to solve problems creatively. Half the battle is just noticing things, saving them for further thought and investigation and connecting them with other things you've noticed.

2. Ask an interesting question.

After making an interesting observation, this should next form an interesting question. These kind of questions usually begin with 'why?'

3. Now form a hypothesis.

A hypothesis is an informed guess as to the possible answer to the question. It may arrive as soon as the question is posed, or it may require a lot of fiddling about. There are often a few different hypotheses. Another word for this is 'ideas'.

4. Conduct experiments.

Ideas must be tested. Bernbach wasn't a fan of pre-testing. Rightly so, if pre-testing worked then everyone would love all the advertising. The best experiment is putting it out into the world.

5. Analyse the data and draw a conclusion.

Here's where we could all do better. We obsess over the wrong data, give disproportionate focus to the insignificant and are distracted by noise. But when we look in the right place then perhaps we have an observation that starts us on the cycle again. Bill was as much scientific as creative. The two fields are not incompatible; they are two sides of the same coin.

Richard Dawkins once pointed out that perhaps the first question aliens would ask upon examining our species is 'Have they figured out evolution yet?' They would have approved of Bill; he was also something of an intuitive evolutionary psychologist.

'It is fashionable to talk about changing man. A communicator must be concerned with unchanging man, with his obsessive drive to survive, to be admired, to succeed, to love, to take care of his own.'

But the money's no good.

Roadrunner twice

I got the modern rockin' neon sound.

While we're on the topic of alien invasions, let's step back in time to October 30, 1938. The Orson Welles radio adaptation of H.G. Wells science fiction novel *War of the Worlds* is playing on CBS Radio's weekly *Mercury Theatre on the Air* show.

Mercury Theatre's regular theme was adapting classic literary works for radio broadcast.

By the late 30's, much of America was adopting the new disruptive technology of radio for their news and entertainment.

As part of the adaptation - and the creative decision to present the play in the form of faux-news bulletins - Welles, his creative partner John Houseman, and writer Howard Koch selected the small town of Grovers Mill (by sticking a pin into a map of New Jersey) to be the site of the alien invasion.

The rest is history, of course. According to lore (and some allegedly scientific analysis - Hadley Cantril's paper *The Invasion from Mars: A Study in the Psychology of Panic* is a notable example) something in the region of one million Americans were sent into blind panic - some keeling over with heart attacks and others committing suicide - all of them certain that New Jersey and America were under attack from Martian invaders.

The reality is a somewhat different story.

Very few listeners were duped by War of the Worlds.

For a start, the audience was pretty small.

Mercury Theatre went out against a long running and hugely popular NBC comedy show playing at the same time slot, which regularly scooped up upwards of 80% of the audience.

Even at the best of times Mercury Theatre accounted for only about 4-5%. Nothing approaching the one million number.

And most of those listeners were well aware that the show's schtick was dramatic radio adaptation.

The stories of widespread panic were actually fabricated, and grossly exaggerated by the newspapers in the following days, most notably by The New York Times.

It turns out that the print media may have been looking for an opportunity to discredit this new emerging channel for news, as they saw radio drama as an imminent threat to their advertising revenue model, and therefore their survival.

So they cooked up a bit of fake news.

Not a bad short-term strategy, it shifted the extra units.

But the threat of death to printed news - or at least the advertising revenue – has never materialised, and the free publicity Mercury Theatre received may even have helped make radio drama seem even sexier, and contributed to an increase popularity. Who knows?

Either way, within 24 months post-War of the Worlds, Welles stock was so high he was able to do a complete-control studio deal with RKO and produce his first feature film, *Citizen Kane*. To this day '…Kane' is widely regarded as one of the greatest movies of all time.

(The newspapers that feared the potential impact the new radio dramas might have on their ad revenue were not thinking about the extra circulation they would ultimately benefit from by reporting on it.)

For all the talk of creativity in business, there's often a disconnect between what people say about creativity and what they unconsciously think. Going into uncharted waters can tend to increase uncertainty.

In 1894 the president of the Royal Society - the UK's national academy of science - Lord Kelvin, confidently predicted that the radio had 'no future'.

The first radio factory was opened 5 years later, and within 8 years a radio set sat in over 50% of US homes.

The time taken to reach 50% of homes is generally accepted as a reasonable way to measure this kind of impact.

And when the transistor was invented in 1947, this ushered in the era of much smaller portable radios.

(American electronics companies showed little interest in developing this nascent idea of portable music so in stepped a Japanese start-up called Sony).

Sony launched the first transistor radio in 1954 and it's no coincidence that rock'n'roll and teenage culture blew up very shortly after.

The aforementioned Lord Kelvin was no stranger to grand - yet spectacularly wrong - predictions.

He was also certain that nothing heavier-than-air would ever fly and that X-rays were simply an elaborate hoax.

These innovations of the early 20th century including electricity, electric light, telephony, TV, radio, central heating, cars and aircraft all had far greater impact on society than digital technologies have had - up to this point.

To use our previous measure, both radio and television were adopted much faster - under 10 years to reach 50% of households - than personal computers or mobile phones at circa 15-17 years respectively.

Funnily enough, many of today's much hyped technologies - smart watches, everything for 'connected' homes, 3D printing and personal robots - are being adopted even more slowly.

This may be because the technology itself is not becoming more disruptive, the majority of the poster children of the digital economy have been services built upon the existing web infrastructure, and we tend to sometimes confuse acceleration with diversification. Digital technology is actually not changing society like never before, nor is the speed of technological change accelerating like never before.

Which is all a shame really, given we are facing a not too distant future of 10billion of us crammed onto a tiny planet without enough food or water.

Meaningful disruption – of the same scale and impact as electricity or the radio in past times – should really be about infrastructure, hygiene, food production, environment and healthcare. Surveillance is sexier, I suppose.

But all is not lost. Because the technology always comes first. Then creative people mess with it and create something new and unexpected. I always attribute this saying to Bill Drummond, but some reckon Lee Clow said it first. Either way it's a good insight.

Try this example. With a disappointing string of flop singles to their name time was running out for fledgling British (off)beat combo The Kinks in 1964.

On the verge of being dumped by Pye Records the producer, Shel Talmy, gifted the lads some left over studio time to record a couple of numbers, with one eye on having some new material to pitch other labels that may want to pick them up.

One of these tunes was a Jimmy Giuffre inspired sax-driven jazzy blues effort titled *You Really Got Me*, brought to the session by the band's leader and chief songwriter Ray Davies.

Even in those early days there was something a sibling rivalry between Ray and his brother Dave, the lead guitarist. Possibly during some *in-the-studio* friction Dave slashed the cone speaker on his Vox AC30 and accidentally discovered the proto-punk/metal distorted guitar sound.

This discovery added some significant oomph when applied to the riff of *You Really Got Me* and transformed what was a fairly pedestrian pseudo r&b knock-off into the genre defining classic, propelling the Kinks from the brink of the beat-boom dustbin to becoming one of the era defining acts alongside the Beatles and the Stones.

Fast-forward to the mid 80's and another accidentally

influential piece of musical tech, The Roland TB-303 Bass Line.

This rudimentary early synth was originally devised as a cheap tool for guitarists who wanted bass accompaniment while honing their licks.

Only about 10,000 units were produced between 1981 and '84, sales were poor, on the surface it looked like a flop product and most remaining units ended up in music store bargain bins.

A few of these discarded synths were picked up by some bootstrapped young DJs and producers in Chicago, among them one Nathan 'DJ Pierre' Jones, who found that by overdriving and cranking the box - using the tool in ways it was never intended to be used - he could manufacture the squelchy 'acid' bass sound.

Shortly after this discovery, DJ Pierre and pals Earl 'Spanky' Smith Jr., and Herbert 'Herb J' Jackson - as 'Phuture' - issued a disco 12" 'Acid Trax' on local Chicago label Trax featuring heavy implementation of the 303 squelch, and a new genre was born.

It's just technology for a while, then when creative people mess around with it things get interesting.

Historically, the advertising business has erred on the side of caution in its adoption of new technology.

The first ever TV ad, a whopping $4 dollar production for Bulova Watches, ran in 1941 but it was almost 20 further years before the industry embraced television as a platform.

Things have speeded up in recent years.

In fact it's been a headfirst dive into digital and social media, then virtual and augmented reality, black boxes of every flavour and now artificial intelligences and machine learning.

As a bonus, with each of these new developments in technology comes the processing of huge amounts of new consumer data - we have more than any other generation of communicators could have even imagined - so it should naturally follow, fully stacked, we can now connect with consumers in better ways than any other generation of marketers could.

Yet it can often feel like more data actually means less. We are even less connected.

Because, in spite of the bluster and gusto, advertising hasn't had a good time figuring out how to make tech, data and creativity work together, and therefore doesn't appear to have a clear articulation of its own future.

Indeed, in most of the industry the conversation is still stuck with another false dilemma.

As if the data-driven and creative are incompatible.

It need not be this way, and we need to resolve this dichotomy fairly urgently.

Data is everywhere, and every day there is more and more data. For many, simply being exposed to the idea of data at this scale is enough to just switch off and become misty-eyed for simpler times, whereas for others the accumulation of data has become something of an end in itself, as if simply possession of the data constitutes a silver bullet.

But the daily reality, for the most part, is more mundane. Agencies may tend to limit their view of data as either, oft times inconvenient, input to inform or rationalise strategic choices, or as, equally inconvenient, output in the form of metrics and measurement.

What's even worse is that during this process they tend to obsess over the wrong data, giving disproportionate focus to small and insignificant differences, get distracted by noise rather than finding the signal, dazzled by vanity metrics and missing the big important things that really matter in guiding strategy.

From that standpoint, any lofty ambitions to assimilate data as a part of the creative process seem a long way off.

Direct marketers and digital marketers will, of course, disagree. They will crow of how they can already effortlessly track and retarget elusive consumers, whilst micro-segmenting audiences and optimising each campaign to within an inch its life.

But is that all there is? Efficiency?

All of the time each of us spends on the internet, and on our smartphones, all the websites we visit, the apps and services we use, everything we buy or think about buying and the people we talk to generates an incredible amount of data on our behaviour and our preferences that could be used by brands to reach consumers. However, just this observation is banal.

Yes, the domination of programmatic delivery, automation and further advertising technology is inevitable. Very soon all media will be bought and distributed in this way. It's a wonderful thing, but the tech, on its own, is not good enough.

We desperately need our best creative minds to grab the opportunity that data and technology provide for creativity. But we need a bridge to connect the two.

To that end, the role for strategic planning in agencies will have to adapt in this new data-rich environment.

While no planners should be strangers to data analysis - some may even have a basic grasp of statistics and recognize a NBD curve when they see it - but the key imperative for strategic thinking in agencies will be to provide the human understanding that connects the data and technology to the creative product.

As a starting point it's worth remembering that any data is really only as useful as the questions asked of it. Data has no intrinsic value.

Understanding what consumers actually do rather than what they say they do is critical. We've learned from the recent advances in behavioural economics and consumer psychology that consumers have, pretty much, no access to the unconscious mental processes that drive most of their decision-making.

However, this doesn't prevent people providing plausible-sounding rationalisations for their behaviour, when asked. Even the process of asking people what they think exerts its own unconscious influence. To the extent that much of the survey data that has traditionally fuelled marketing decision making is, at worst, a total fiction or at best only an artefact of the research process, itself.

The consumer psychologist Philip Graves famously channelled Edgar Allen Poe by remarking 'trust nothing consumers say, about half of what we see them do, and nearly everything the sales data tells us they have done'.

Graves is adamant that real sales data and covert behavioural observation should always be the start point of any research.

The use of the words 'covert observation' can quickly divide a room. However when the focus of any research is overt - the participants are aware of what's being investigated - then, while it feels like it's more transparent or 'ethical' this research is mostly useless. Knowing one's behaviour is being observed is intrinsically biasing. When people are aware that they are being observed they become more self-conscious and their behaviour changes.

This is where the new developments in data technology might become interesting.

Artificial Intelligence and Machine Learning are two buzz phrases being used right now - often interchangeably - but they are not quite the same thing. For our purposes as advertisers, it's enough to know that one is effectively an application of the other.

Machine Learning, then, is a particular application of one AI based around the idea that - given access to enough data - machines can learn for themselves. Put simply, a machine learning AI is essentially a system fuelled by algorithms, and as these algorithms are exposed to new data they teach themselves and grow.

Basic machine learning applications can read and interpret text (making inferences about the tone of the text it is reading), all programmatic ad trading is applied AI, chuck in other applications like self-driving cars, Siri and rudimentary speech recognition and a lot of this kind of applied AI is all around us, now. But these examples are what the boffins would label 'narrow' AI.

Narrow or not, these developments are reasonably impressive from the technology standpoint and present a platform for creative people to do something new and unexpected.

In simple terms, the benefit lies in the ability to identify an individual node, rather than trying to make sense of multiple cookies and multiple devices that may be associated with an individual. It is not about micro-targeting and extreme personalization, this 'narrow' view (to borrow the technical jargon of our AI engineer friends) is just more of the Peppers and Rogers circular logic.

AIs are going to be far more useful in accurately sizing markets, uncovering the real sales and behavioural data and the necessary covert behavioural observation that allows us to group together bigger sets of consumers through shared insights.

Advertisers should be interested in observing these network effects. As anyone with even a basic understanding of simple network theory will tell you, the value of a network increases as it grows bigger. A simple applied description of machine learning with personal information is described nicely for the lay person (or advertising practitioner) Kevin Kelly's 2017 book *The Inevitable* and in the chapter on 'Cognifying' (one of the 12 tech forces that he predicts will be the most important in the next couple of decades).

The more people who use an AI, the smarter it gets. The smarter it gets, the more people who use it, the more people who use it, the smarter it gets. And so on'

Kelly describes a moment in 2002 when this became clear to him. While making conversation with assorted engineers at a private party within Google HQ he came to the realisation that we had been looking at our Silicon Valley overlords ultimate goals the wrong way round. Google were not interested in the application of AIs to make their core products like search better, it was OUR usage of search that was feeding Google's AIs. Google was fundamentally an AI company.

Our usage feeds the AI. The more we use it the smarter it gets, and so on.

Today, smartphone data is obviously they key - about 90% of all these devices are uniquely identifiable with an individual - we can infer almost the total composition of any audience, as well as where, when, with what and with whom media is used. Almost all category entry points in one fell swoop. And the full-tilt expansion of personal media means that the near future promises new technologies with capabilities far beyond the abilities of our smartphones.

The mainstreaming of machine learning capabilities, will provide agencies with better building blocks for smarter campaigns, and constitutes something of a leap in marketing intelligence, but as we've noted before, simply turbo-boosting targeting and delivery of ads is not where the real potential for AI applications in communications lies.

Even adding the benefit of population level behavioural data and insights we are still working with 'narrow' AIs.

Things start to get much more interesting when we can map human psychology onto the data.

We live in a modern world of complex social networks. We interact with hundreds of people each day, in both physical and virtual environments. Success in this environment means being best adapted to interacting with, and working with other people and getting what you want from others.

Each of us has things that annoy us and things that make us happy. Our minds become very skilled good at remembering other people's preferences and they, ours.

This skill evolved long ago in our ancestral past, one of many adaptations that shaped our minds into the way they are because these adaptations enabled our stone-age ancestors to succeed with their (and our) principal concerns, namely survival, reproducing, competing and forming mutually beneficial alliances.

But we are limited by our cognitive capacity. It takes a huge amount of cognitive effort to remember other people's preferences. But the pay-offs are there when we get it right.

When the anthropologist Robin Dunbar was trying to solve the problem of why primates (including humans) and other social species devote so much time and effort to this kind of 'grooming' behaviour, he happened upon his eponymous number.

Dunbar's number (around 150) described a theoretical limit to the number of people with whom any individual is able to sustain a stable or meaningful social relationship.

150 is a best case number and even in the age of digital social networks, the number of friends with whom you keep in touch, and groom, is likely to be less than Dunbar's number.

But for brands, companies and institutions - for whom the Holy Grail is to sustain stable relationships, keep in touch with and groom literally millions of consumers - the really big opportunities that the harnessing the tsunami of personally identifiable data and the power machine learning and other AI applications offer lie in these areas.

The ability to manage relationships with and remember the

(often implicit and unarticulated) preferences, of millions of individuals with the same intimacy as these tight-knit groups of humans manage their own relationships, is the bridge that could finally connect the technology, the data and the creativity.

Curiously, old dumb media was far better at providing appropriate 'context' for advertising than the new smart media has. In simple terms, a planner could pick which shows, pages or environments the ads would appear in.

But, some sort of AI driven programmatic system that properly senses the context or environment would be a simple application that could improve placement and performance of web and mobile ads, with dynamic creative.

Following this thought I went to see some techno boffins to validate. 'We can already do all of that', they replied. 'But creative agencies and planners are too lazy to do the work needed to implement it, or even to ask'. But context is as important as content in many respects, perhaps more so than we have credited.

In experiments conducted by psychologists Kenrick and Griskevicius, the pair showed groups different movies and measured responses. Some were shown scary films like *The Shining*, Stanley Kubrick's terrifying adaptation of the equally terrifying Stephen King novel and others were shown soppy drama like *Before Sunrise* starring Ethan Hawke and Julie Delpy.

The responses to the movies were unimportant, what was really being examined - covertly - were the responses to variants of two ads for a Las Vegas Art museum placed in the ad breaks.

In the first version of the museum ad the end line was 'Visited by over a million people a year', a *herding* or popularity tactic. In the second the message was 'Stand out from the crowd', appealing to the viewers sense of independent choice or uniqueness.

It turns out that the herding message was received more favourably by those respondents who saw *The Shining*. Whilst the standing out message resonated more with the *Before Sunrise* groups.

The authors hypothesised that being primed with fear can nudge people towards seeking safety in numbers – activating a *self-protection* module - but priming with romantic notions can encourage people to want to want to demonstrate their individuality, and unique attractiveness – activating the *mate-acquisition* module.

That consumer preferences are not fixed is fairly well established but it turns out we can have markedly different preferences from one moment to the next. There should be an

AI for that.

I'm carried by Kevin Kelly's optimism, when he proposes, 'There is almost nothing we can think of that cannot be made new, different, or interesting by infusing it with some extra IQ. In fact, the business plans of the next 10,000 startups are easy to forecast: Take X and add AI.'

Take market research and add AI.

Take consumer psychology and add AI.

Take creativity and add AI.

If all this sounds a bit cheerful, as ever there's a dark side. Whatever advertisers are doing with these new data processing techniques is probably the least of anyone's worries.

The bad news is that nefarious data brokers are already using sophisticated algorithms to observe patterns in society and behaviour and create information useful to the likes of insurance firms and banks.

Someone significantly more dangerous that the average advertising douchebag can already infer the likelihood of thousands of details that you may never have wittingly revealed.

Religion, political views, health, personality traits and economic stability amongst hundreds of others.

These inferences are called 'derived data', the property of

the collector, protected by law and far more coveted than 'your data', like email addresses or phone numbers.

Whenever a third party collector claims they don't sell your data, that doesn't mean they are not selling theirs.

There's an old saying that goes along these lines; there are only two groups of people whose movements are continuously monitored.

The first group are monitored involuntarily by order of the courts or suchlike with tracking devices attached to their person.

The second group is everybody else.

Perhaps if we can work towards *us* watching government and corporations as much as corporations and government watch us then there's mutual value to be had.

Everyone will be familiar with the words of the data-scientist W. Edwards Deming who asserts 'Without data you are just another person with an opinion'.

In our business there are no shortage of opinions.

Deming, quite rightly, demands the objective facts. And we have more facts and data at our disposal than at any time in human history.

However to complete the picture, and to take the opportunity that data and technology give for creativity, I propose an addendum to Deming's thesis.

Without data you are just another person with an opinion? Correct.

But, without a coherent model of human behaviour, you are just another AI with data.

Machine learning and AIs offer us much more than just the better mousetraps of targeting and delivery. The big opportunity is for understanding what people value, why they behave the way they do, and *how* people are thinking (rather than just *what*).

This could bring new, previously hidden, perspectives to inform both the construction of creative interventions and deeper understanding exactly where, when and how these interventions will have the most power.

Psycho junk food

Even better than the real thing?

Is the internet rewiring the brains of millennials, as they *evolve* and *adapt* to the new processing skills they need to survive in today's information saturated environment?

And, among the essential adaptations are there new abilities evolving for things like rapid searching, assessing quality, and synthesizing vast quantities of information and data?

Well, some pundits even go as far as to add that an ability to think about one thing in isolation, in any depth, will be of far less consequence for most people in the near future, therefore contributing to new social divides and labour divides between these new evolved 'supertaskers' and the previous generation of dullards.

(If you can't think once, then don't think twice.)

On the other hand, is it the case that the internet has produced a generation addicted to quick-fixes of info-nuggets, self-obsessed, averse to any critical analysis, making shallow choices and chasing instant gratification?

There's not much wrong with that description either, except there's nothing particularly new or adapted to behold, and it certainly wasn't the product of the internet.

It's a fairly standard illustration of young human behaviour throughout the ages.

I prefer the explanation offered by Steven Pinker.

'Claims that the Internet is changing human thought are propelled by a number of forces: the pressure on pundits to announce that this or that 'changes everything'; a superficial conception of what 'thinking' is that conflates content with process…The most interesting trend in the development of the Internet is not how it is changing people's ways of thinking but how it is adapting to the way that people think.'

Human biological evolution solves only 'adaptive' problems, the kind that concern surviving long enough to successfully pass on our genes into the next generation.

Among these problems are those concerning what to eat and avoiding getting eaten, finding the best quality mating partners, collaborating and competing with each other for status and resources.

These are the kinds of problems that were the most common in the 'environment of evolutionary adaptedness' - the stone age hunter-gatherer environment our ancestors navigated - not our modern world of technology, media, celebrities and consumerism.

It was during this time - that's approximately 99% of human existence, the stone age lasted for a couple of million years - that our minds did almost all of their evolving. A time when we lived in small groups of maybe only a few dozen people gathering plants and hunting animals.

Our modern world is a tiny, tiny blip in comparison.

We've only had agriculture for about 10,000 years, the industrial revolution was just over 200 years ago and the internet has only been around for about 20 years. Not nearly enough time has elapsed for our minds to adapt to these new conditions. Our modern minds are designed for solving ancient stone age problems, not for dealing with the *supernormal stimuli* of the 21st century.

Even very simple challenges can stump our stone age minds. The Wason Selection Task, developed by the cognitive psychologist Peter Wason in 1966, demonstrates how it can be extraordinarily difficult to solve an abstract, numerical modern world problem, but far easier when the same challenge is posed as a social exchange problem - like one our stone-age ancestors would have faced.

Imagine you've got the task of sorting out 4 cards correctly. The cards are laid out flat, with each displaying a character or number. D, F, 3 and 7 respectively.

The puzzle is this; if tell you that when a card has a 'D' on one side, it must have '3' on the other side. Which cards do you have to turn over in order to see if this is true?

Most people will choose D and 3, but the correct answer is D and 7.

If a card with a D on one side it must have a 3 on the other is not the same as saying a card with a 3 must have a D on the other side.

So whether the 3 has a D on its other side or not is irrelevant, you need to know what's on the other side of the 7.

While you're puzzling that one, think about it this way.

For this one, you must imagine you are a bouncer in a club and must find the under-age drinkers. The club rule is that only over 18's can drink beer. The cards each represent individual punters and have an age on one side and drink on the other - 18, 25, beer, Coke.

Most people have no problem selecting the right cards (16 and beer). So why is it that people are far better with drinks and ages than with letters and numbers? Both tests are logically exactly the same.

Because in the bouncer problem, your 'cheat-detection' mental module kicks in.

Human social exchanges, and those of many other animals, work along the lines of tit-for-tat. Or 'you scratch my back...' In the ancestral environment it made survival sense to be pretty good at keeping a check of who owes who what – and at spotting and punishing cheaters. A particular set of mental processes evolved for this purpose, and they still come in pretty handy today. Although, like in any arms race, it gets harder to spot the cheats as faking techniques and technologies improve (I only add this point in case readers think we've gone off-topic...)

Most of what we fear also has an evolutionary basis. Snakes, spiders, heights, thunder, lightning, the dark, blood, strangers are just a few. No one has to be taught these innate fears. Yet the things in the modern world that we really should be afraid of – climbing into a tin can and then propelling oneself around at high speed surrounded by hundreds of other maniacs in their tin cans) - are not particularly frightening to most of us, even though this activity kills far more people in a day than snakes or spiders do in a decade.

I've argued in the past for using road signs featuring enormous Redback Spiders or Tiger Snakes in road safety campaigns. Pulling on a fear that reaches into our evolutionary past, evoking an ancient, instinctive reaction with *supernormal stimuli*. One day it will fly.

The theory of *supernormal stimulus* was developed in the

1950s by biologist and ornithologist Nikolaas 'Niko' Tinbergen. He found that biologically salient objects, like beaks and eggs, generated more interest from his bird subjects when they were painted, pimped and blown up in size.

In one experiment herring gull chicks pecked more at big red knitting needles than adult herring gull beaks, because they were bigger and redder and longer than real beaks.

A young student of Tinbergen called Richard Dawkins experimented with male stickleback fish and supernormal dummy females. The real female sticklebacks naturally swell up when they are fertile and full of eggs.

By making his dummy female fish much bigger and rounder than normal the males became more attracted to the dummies. Dawkins is credited with introducing 'sex bomb' into the lexicon in describing this example.

A Supernormal stimulus is what Bono might describe as 'even better than the real thing'.

Evolution has designed male Australian jewel beetles go after for cues of shiny amber-brown surfaces with the presence of dimples, as these were almost certain to be female beetles. This normal stimulus triggered a normal adaptive behaviour. But Australian beer bottles - stubbies - give off these exact same cues, only much bigger and shinier.

They are everywhere in the male beetles' environment and

the males are getting distracted. Beer bottles are super-normal stimuli for male beetles, triggering a maladaptive behaviour.

Of course, many animals exaggerate features to attract mates, mimic other species or protect themselves against predators. But these changes happen slowly over evolutionary time. Supernormal is a term that can be used to describe any stimulus that elicits a response stronger than the stimulus for which it evolved.

Junk food is a super stimulus version of real food to humans. Things like sugar and fat, that were biologically salient, but scarce in the stone-age environment, are all around us, in abundance, every day. But it's not just the external cues that are super-normal, but the internal rewards too. A Big Mac gives you a bumper hit of sugar, fat, and flavour far more intensely than a bowl of rolled oats or boiled cabbage.

Oscar Wilde famously stated 'I can resist everything but temptation'.

None of us can. Stuffing our faces with calories, drinking and taking drugs, gambling, obsessing over the lives of celebrities whom we are never likely to meet, competing for status at the office and generally wasting time with people who wouldn't care if we lived or died rather than spending time with our families. These are just a few examples of common, and maladaptive, behaviours.

Of course, all of those new temptations mentioned are hard to resist, because in the world our minds evolved to inhabit they didn't exist. They are supernormal stimuli that elicit a response stronger than the stimuli for which their response mechanisms evolved.

Our Silicon Valley overlords, however, now have the cultural tools that allow us to consciously manipulate these signals in real time, and the makers of these tools know this very well.

If you were the planner in an ad agency anytime between 1965 and about 10 years ago, your work was fairly straightforward. You would do your research, find some insights and – if you were any good – develop an interesting platform that the creatives could jump from to make the ads.

But the sexier modern advertising environment has raised our reward thresholds. The old rewards just don't *synergise 24-7 mindshare*, do they? Our new *blockchain content glasses* are a super-normal stimulus causing maladaptive behaviours.

The super successful products of the digital economy like Facebook, Twitter, Tinder, Instagram are all supernormal stimuli. They work so well because they are perfectly adapted to create supernormal stimuli for our stone-age minds. We are wired to compete for status among our peers in the small groups on the savannahs we used to inhabit. But now we can compete with millions of strangers on the internet.

So, the next time you hear about how the internet is rewiring our brains, it's really the internet adapting to and exploiting how our brains work.

Rather than being an all-purpose information processor, the mind consists of a number of specialised 'modules', or apps, designed by evolution to cope with certain recurring adaptive problems. The mind's 'apps' are specific processes that evolved in response to our ancestral environment. Our minds have apps for mating behaviour, gossip, looking out for family members, making deals with strangers, personality traits and so on. The successful products of the digital economy are the ones that mirror and exaggerate these response mechanisms. What's modern is in our environment, not in our minds. And an OS update takes thousands of generations to load.

So for your next disruptive innovation idea, just find a super-stimulating version of a natural reward. But make it sexier, cuter, sweeter, bigger, louder or with more teeth.

There's a free strategy for you. Off you go.

Psychological junk food.

Although, AI robot sex dolls is already becoming a crowded category.

Gimme gimme shock treatment

And the Rosser Reeves fallacy.

So much for biological salience, but salience - in the marketing sense - refers to the likelihood that a particular brand will 'come to mind' easily in buying situations.

In *How Brands Grow*, Professor Byron Sharp uses 'salience' to further describe the idea of 'mental availability'.

The easier a brand is to remember, in more buying situations, for more potential buyers, then the higher the overall mental 'availability' of the brand, ergo the more likelihood that the most salient brand will be bought.

And salience is also widely used in cognitive science, to describe the attention grabbing quality of things in general.

This is where ad people often get confused. While a campaign may be salient in the cognitive sense - its content is eye catching or entertaining for example - its effectiveness as a branding vehicle depends of how easily it is for those who view or interact will 'remember' which brand it was at an appropriate buying opportunity.

This requires subconscious (and conscious) brand cues throughout, fuelling the 'content-addressable memory'.

Computers are binary with a numerically ordered and numbered memory. If it wants to find something it goes to a specific address and picks up the piece of information.

This is known as byte-addressable memory.

But brain chemistry runs on content addressable memory or associative memory.

The big difference is that when a memory is piqued in the human mind a signal is sent to the entire memory and those memory locations that have a scrap of related information all respond at once.

This is why familiar and popular brands become salient in buying or usage contexts - the number and quality of associations is strong enough to bring the brand 'to mind'.

Therefore ad salience and brand salience are two halves of the same job yet much branded material will routinely fail on both these points.

It's neither ad 'salient' (i.e. it might be pitched as 'comedic' but nowhere near as funny as regular unbranded comedy therefore does not stand-out) nor is it brand salient (assuming one has the mettle to stick it out through 90 seconds of sub standard 'entertainment' the branding itself may fleetingly appear only on the end frame).

Certain mental health conditions such as psychosis and schizophrenia are also now widely believed to involve, at least in part, a problem with the mind's regulation of salience. In states of psychosis ordinary or commonplace things appear more important or alarming than they should. In extreme cases this can take the form of delusions or hallucinations.

More than just being mistaken or perhaps causing mild confusion they can include disturbing states such as believing that your thoughts are being manipulated by aliens, external forces are controlling your actions, or believing that people want to engage in meaningful relationships with brands.

This idea, 'psychosis as a state of aberrant salience' was popularised by the psychiatrist Shitij Kapur.

Kapur's *Aberrant Salience Theory* connects delusions and hallucinations to differences in dopamine function.

He argues that dopamine is crucial in highlighting which things are 'motivationally important', how they stand out from each other.

Dopamine plays a critical role in the function of the central nervous system, and is also linked with the brain's complex system of motivation and reward.

Dopamine release can be artificially stimulated through the

use of drugs like MDMA (ecstasy), whereas instances where dopamine release would naturally occur include when your football team wins the Premiership (I'm an Aberdeen FC supporter so I've only small memory fragments of what that feels like), hugging your child, or when a Twitter campaign delivers a 1500% ROI.

At least one of advertising's own manifestations of Aberrant Salience can be traced back to Rosser Reeves.

In 1934, the young Reeves left his small town home in Danville, Virginia, for the bright lights of New York City, following his dream of working as an advertising copywriter.

Within a few years he had landed a plum job at the Ted Bates Advertising Agency and by 1950 he was vice-president and head of copy, rising to chairman of the board in 1955.

Then in 1961 he published his first book *Reality of Advertising*, a large portion of which was devoted to Reeves's principal legacy (and the 'secret' to the phenomenal success of Bates in the 1950s) - the unique selling proposition (USP).

(Incidentally, the Don Draper character from Mad Men is generally agreed to be an amalgam of several of the leading ad figures of the time, including Reeves.

George Lois and Draper Daniels are the others most often referenced.)

Anyway, Reeves defined a USP has having three main parts. Each ad must contain a proposition - 'Buy Brand X and you get this specific benefit'. The proposition must be unique to the brand - something that competitors can't offer. The proposition must sell - it must be something that will, for example, persuade consumers to switch brands.

To this day the requirement for and persuasive power of a USP is perhaps the most commonly held belief in agencies of all flavours.

Almost any variant of a creative brief will contain box for the 'proposition'. Or the 'one-thing-we-must-say'.

It sounds confident and plausible, but the truth of the matter is that the idea of a USP was simply something Reeves made up, was based on exactly zero evidence, no research and - as Paul Feldwick points out in his *Anatomy of Humbug* (a must-read for those with an interest in the history of these matters) - not even on a semi-coherent theory.

Why would he do such a thing?

Slightly less well known is that propagating the USP notion was a deliberate strategy employed to distance his agency, from a more dangerous accusation being touted by journo Vance Packard via his 1957 book *The Hidden Persuaders* which had become a surprise best-seller.

Packard's investigation 'revealed' for the first time the

psychological manipulations and mind control employed by the evil ad industry - aided by 'foreign' psychologists and their 'subliminal advertising techniques - in order to make Americans buy stuff they didn't need nor want.

This fear was possibly a lingering by-product of the Cold War with Russia that had unfolded from the late 1940s, fuelling concern that America was being infiltrated by communism - the 'reds under the bed' - and their nefarious mind-control programs.

Reeves was clear in his point of view. 'There are no hidden persuaders. Advertising works openly, in the bare and pitiless sunlight.'

In a way Reeves's USP notion may simply have been a counter-strategy designed to defend the Bates agency against the scare tactics of the likes of Packard. He didn't believe in it particularly, but if it got the 'investigative' journalists off the scent then it was all good.

Yet the USP prevails to this day and, what's more, it has spawned several other equally un-quantified yet stated-as-fact marketing theories like 'differentiation', 'positioning' and 'loyalty beyond reason'.

Sadly, consumers are not up to speed with these theories and tend to buy popular brands they have heard of and/or used before. And brand loyalty - while it absolutely exists in all categories – is, for the most part, a simplification strategy employed by consumers to avoid having to think too much rather than having anything to do with devotion.

Many marketers still also believe that changing customer retention rates is cheaper than improving customer acquisition, and that asking customers their likelihood of recommending the brand is a predictor of brand growth.

This Net Promoter Score System was devised by Frederick Reichheld of Bain & Co, also responsible for the debunked but still widely believed myth that a five per cent drop in customer defections leads to 80 per cent plus increase in profits.

There is actually zero scientific evidence to credit any of these theories and yet they are widely believed to be facts.

In the year or so I spent working in 'content marketing' I encountered another curious idea.

It was pretty much written in stone (the content marketing tablets, brought down from the mount, somewhere near Cleveland) that native advertising or sponsored content should not explicitly promote or reference the brand sponsoring the piece.

This was believed by practitioners to be overly 'shilling' or inauthentic, and therefore will be rejected by readers as 'advertising'.

But is there any evidence to support this view?

A report commissioned by AOL and presented at ESOMAR Congress Dublin in September 2015 titled *What Normative Data says about Effectiveness* investigated brand sponsored content (native/advertorial) within Huffington Post and some of AOL's other many digital publishing properties.

In carefully designed double-blind experiments, and in scrutinising the subsequent data, author Christian Kugel came to the surprising conclusion that:

'Not only do activations with heavier brand integration perform better to drive higher recall and consideration, the content itself is also rated directionally more favourably.

One would expect that content with less brand presence would be more favourable, so the fact that this shows an equivalent measure is excellent news for brands as well as publishers involved in content marketing. It means that we do not have to be afraid to push for heavier brand presence and integration. It is a fascinating revelation and a counter-intuitive insight coming out of the data.'

Kugel was somewhat surprised with his findings in the area of content marketing and sponsored content but they do seem to correspond with what we've already understood from the science of 'viral' video space thanks to Dr Karen Nelson-Field.

In her 2013 report *Viral Marketing*, Nelson-Field found

there was no detrimental impact on how much sharing across the social web a video achieved relating to the level of branding used.

Not only that, the evidence suggested that overt branding has no impact on a video's ability to illicit an emotional response.

These findings also ran counter to the content marketing industry's conventional 'wisdom', which suggests removing branding or keeping it to an absolute minimum.

'It turns out that consumers have a higher threshold than many practitioners initially assumed', says Christian Kugel.

It also turns out that a lot of what the industry believes is based on assumption, received wisdom and a complicated set of Chinese whispers dating as far back as the 1940s.

Just because certain beliefs are popular, doesn't mean they are right and this situation isn't helpful for poor modern brand marketers. Let's not forget they are grappling with all kinds of new problems in 2017, many more than their predecessors in past decades.

These new problems include making sense of the perceived threat of 'digital disruption', 'big data', navigating the implications of programmatic media buying and getting their heads around the ever-growing number of channels available to potentially reach consumers.

Luckily, recent developments in marketing science and behavioural science are giving us a much better view of how categories typically behave, models to better understand the patterns that underpin what people buy and the types of strategies buyers use to simplify buying decisions.

And it turns out that creativity and science are much better friends than many would have you believe.

The principle objection to scientific marketing ideas seems to come from creative quarters, who still associate 'science' and Rosser Reeves claims, the one's he made to bail Bates out from the Packard driven *inquisition*.

'I warn you against believing that advertising is a science', said Bill Bernbach, the anti-Reeves.

My sense is that if Bill were around today he would be embracing the marketing science for the space it creates for free creativity.

There is a final passage in the influential paper entitled *Brand Advertising as Creative Publicity* by Rachel Kennedy, Andrew Ehrenberg et al, published in the Journal of Advertising Research in 2002, which would almost certainly have tickled Bernbach.

The authors propose that brand advertising seems to work best by simply creatively publicising a brand (salience), and not by trying to persuade people that the brand differs from other brands, or is even better or best.

'Some people fear that this 'mere publicity' stance is unhelpful to creatives. But we suggest that the exact opposite is the case.

But having to centre your advertising on adding year after year some indiscernible 'Whiter and Brighter' product-boon can restrict the kind of creativity that aims at memorable impacts for the brand.

In contrast, publicizing a brand gives ample scope for imaginative insights and for disciplined marketing communication skills.

This can stimulate creativity, making distinctive and memorable publicity for the brand out of next to nothing. This seems the hallmark of good advertising, as we know it.

There is huge scope - the campaign need not be hemmed in by the brand's 'selling proposition.'

German psychologist Gerd Gigerenzer calls upon 'recognition heuristics' - another way of describing salience and creative publicity.

'Firms that spend their money on buying space in your recognition memory know this. Similarly politicians advertising their names and faces rather than their policies, wannabe celebrities, and even small nations operate on the principle that if we do not recognise them, we will not favour them. Taken to the extreme, [just] being recognised becomes the goal in itself'

Indeed, Gigerenzer even offers a specific smart recognition heuristic for buying hi-fi equipment with minimum effort, just choose a brand you recognize and go for the second least expensive model. A smart heuristic.

To be fair to old Rosser Reeves, you know you've made it when they name a logical fallacy after you. Just like his USP the 'Rosser Reeves Fallacy' still prevails on research agencies to this day, you probably hear some variant every week.

Reeves' research 'method' famously showed that when consumers were 'aware' of his client's ads they were more favourably disposed towards those clients' brands across a range of measures, including likelihood to buy.

This clearly showed that *his* advertising was more effective! Rosser's clients lapped this up but the logic is, of course, fatally flawed. Buyers of any given brand have a higher awareness of a brand's advertising than non-buyers.

We tend to remember those brands we like, are familiar with and use. So rather than those aware of the ads being more likely to buy the brand, it's actually those who buy the brand being more aware of the ads. Cause and effect the wrong way round (again).

No room to rhumba!

The natural selection of interesting.

It can legitimately be said that Elvis Presley probably made more terrible records than any other artist in history.

The appalling *There's No Room to Rhumba in a Sports Car* - from the soundtrack of 1963's *Fun In Acapulco* turkey - is certainly one.

But also true is that he also made more truly great records than just about anyone else. The vast majority of the horrible Elvis records were made during his bad movie period of 1960 to 67, immediately following his stint in the army.

But the crucial and pivotal moment for Elvis has become known as his '68 Comeback Special'.

The show, simply titled *Elvis*, went out on December 3, 1968 on the NBC television network.

The back-to-basics and black leather clad Elvis hooked up with some old band mates from the 56-58 vintage years period in a stripped down rock'n'roll jam session, interspersed with a nod to the 'future' grown-up Elvis oeuvre via bigger soulful numbers like *In The Ghetto* and the epic *If I Can Dream*.

But here's the question.

Was it, in fact, a necessary process for Elvis to go through that period of creative failure during 60-67 in order to come out the other side bigger bolder and stronger?

In *The Origins of Genius* the psychologist Dean Simonton argues that creativity can best be understood as a Darwinian process of variation and selection.

The successful artist generates a ton of ideas, subjects those ideas to some sort of evaluation criteria, then lets loose only those bets that look promising (those that appear to have the best chances of survival and reproductive *fitness*).

Then some do and some don't. Nevertheless, the true measure of creative genius is the passing on of an influential body of work to future generations. Although, as we shall discuss, this will only be evident in hindsight.

Simonten argues that 'Quality, is a probabilistic function of quantity'.

Taking up this argument, it may indeed follow that the simple difference between Elvis and the thousands of one-hit-wonders or wannabe rock'n'rollers that amounted to nothing much in the fifties and sixties isn't necessarily that he had a better ratio of hits to misses.

The difference is that the mediocre might have a few half-decent ideas, whereas Elvis was exponentially more prolific in his output.

Because Elvis put out such a vast number of 'experiments' it was almost inevitable that some would end up being great.

Simonton's point is that there is nothing neat and efficient about creativity.

The more successes there are, the more failures there are as well'.

The creative person who can pump out more ideas than the rest of us will have far more bad ideas than the rest of us, too. But, critically, they will probably also have more good ideas.

Fluctuation in fortune is 'regression to the mean'.

In the case of Elvis, the 60-67 mediocrity blip was indeed a blip.

A strange outcome is usually followed by something much more ordinary.

Unpredictable events (i.e. Army service) disrupted the average quality of output, then in '68 normal service resumed.

It's popular to talk about 'vulnerability' in advertising – this notion that campaigns could go either way and total disaster is but a whisker away from outrageous success.

This is somewhat true, *individual* successes are hard - perhaps impossibly hard - to predict.

It's only after-the-fact that it seems to be clear why something took off.

A more recent pop example is South Korean rapper and producer Psy. When Psy and his crew were in the studio cranking out *Gangnam Style* in 2012, no way were they strategising for a global phenomenon.

They were hoping for another hit in South Korea, where he was already huge.

If it had flopped globally then it wouldn't have been the end of the world.

Similarly, Psy knows that his chances of ever repeating the unprecedented phenomenon of *Gangnam Style* are extremely unlikely.

Upon being quizzed about how his personal view of the success of 'Gangnam Style' and whether he felt under pressure to follow it up with something else of a comparable scale, Psy claimed he was fine with success, and was 6 big albums into a very successful pop career in his native South Korea.

But, he added, Gangnam Style was not 'success'.

It was actually a phenomenon.

And that that this phenomenon actually had very little to

do with Psy, himself, and almost everything to do with its adoption by everyone else.

So as well as contributing his piece to the 'folk' tradition, or publicly 'owned' culture, even if no-one outside of South Korea hears of PSY again he has also nicely framed 'Gangnam Style' as a special case rather than one-hit wonder, and can then go back to simply being a huge success.

It's important that we understand this in advertising, embracing unpredictability, not getting carried away with huge successes and not worry too much about the odd flop.

But for an advertiser or agency who have the working practices in place that allow them to continually produce quality, they should expect to be able continue to produce quality, if they stay on their game.

One creative department I worked with operated on this principle (perhaps intuitively, or perhaps there were unspoken Darwinian philosophies at play).

At the end of each day creative teams would file in to present their work to the creative leadership.

They might well have been presenting the greatest idea in the history of advertising but would almost inevitably be sent away to improve it or come back with further ideas the next day. Nothing got by on first (or even second) pass.

If there was time then the work could always be made better.

If there wasn't time, the suits would make it their business to buy time.

In this spirit, the '68 Special highpoint, *If I Can Dream* was actually written overnight (at the request of Elvis himself) the night before the recording of the show, by the King's musical director Walter Earl Brown.

The number was a last-minute replacement for a schmaltzy Christmas number that Elvis's manager, Colonel Parker, had originally wanted.

But the King put his foot down, and 'Dream' became effectively Elvis' post-rock'n'roll career defining moment.

Mediocrity produces fewer ideas, every now and again one may get lucky, but regression to the mean would indicate that the hits will be few and the majority will be like *No Room to Rhumba in a Sports Car.*

A Darwinian creative approach means producing more ideas, more often knowing the best of them will survive and reproduce.

Quality is a probabilistic function of quantity.

Thursday's rags

From the Velvets to the void.

In 1967 the biggest selling and most popular US album was *More of the Monkees*. Extremely popular, umpteen millions of copies sold.

Also released in 1967 was The Velvet Underground's first album *The Velvet Underground and Nico*.

The Velvets never troubled the top 100 album chart with this, or any of their subsequent albums, but nigh on every one of the brave souls who witnessed a Velvets performance or purchased the album went on to form their own bands or become painters, or artists of some description.

And over the long game the Velvets and Lou ultimately outsold the Monkees, indeed Lou's *Transformer* is as much an iconic punk document as anything else of the time, even though it's from '72.

In my first punky band as a teenager the bass player's art teacher force-fed us *Transformer*, along with The Stooges *Funhouse*, The Mothers of Invention's *Freak Out* (somewhat out of left-field, it must be said) alongside bits of John

Coltrane, Sun Ra and other assorted weirdness. We tended to draw the line after The Mothers. I've flirted with jazz in odd moments of pretentiousness over the subsequent years but it's never stuck.

Later, as a young art student in the mid-80s that first Velvets album was a permanent 'under the arm' fixture in the art school corridors - for signalling purposes and as a *fitness* indicator, obviously.

I also recall petitioning the art materials shop within the college to stock the album, as an essential material for new students, along with their paints and canvas.

The 'influence' of the Velvets can still be felt as it has permeated right through much of the important music from the late 60s to now.

In 1967 nobody knew that the Velvets were going to be influential. They were one of many New York groups that emerged as an antithesis to West Coast hippie-dom. Their influence was only apparent later on.

Because the true measure of 'influence' is what happens next. How the idea propagates through networks. How people adopt an idea to go and do something with it.

But we can only identify this with hindsight.

Somehow we've got a little bit confused about the nature of

influence in marketing.

The idea that brands can pick out and target a small group of social media users - or 'authentic creators', to use the correct technical term, ahem - with their large 'followings' and then imagine that they will direct everyone else is still prevalent however this influencer theory is a myth and its protagonists have got things the wrong way round.

There are a couple of reasons marketers still like to believe in this idea of the 'influencers'.

Firstly, a little bit of laziness. It's a lot easier to believe that a message can spread by the brand tapping apparently popular individuals - those special few to whom we all turn to in order to make decisions as Gladwellian thinking would have it - rather than get down with the messy business of continually reaching a mass of distracted, disinterested consumers.

Secondly, just by implementing these 'influencer' strategies it's actually the brands themselves who appear to be the ultra influentials!

They, after all, are now the ones who influence the influencers.

Sadly neither of these things is true

What is true, is that you're just as likely to spread a message or product by targeting a mass market of random consumers as you would by going after so-called influencers, as long as the conditions are right.

If people are ready to adopt a product, message or trend, then just about anybody can start one, but if the conditions aren't right, then no one can.

Indeed, most of what we should call real influence is much more accidental and principally involves easily influenced people influencing other easily influenced people, without either party being particularly cognisant of the influence.

There's bad news and good news.

The bad news is that the specific conditions in which any given trend might emerge are very hard to predict and success only looks like success in hindsight.

The good news is that the psychology literature explains the general conditions for copying behaviour pretty well.

All day long people unconsciously mimic the behaviours of others they interact with, including facial expressions, accents, postures, gestures, mannerisms and emotions. And the simple act of observing others' behaviour can induce behavioural mimicry, particularly the behaviour of others who appear similar to us, and all of the above are unconscious automatic processes.

Likewise, simply observing others' choices induces choice

mimicry - just like behavioural mimicry it occurs automatically - and collectively when we are uncertain about which behaviours or choices are acceptable or accurate, then we use a consensus heuristic to be on the safe side.

Or in more simple terms, ordinary people copy other ordinary people without really noticing they are doing it.

My good friend Mark Earls, who kindly penned the foreword for this book, has written and spoken extensively on these matters, and the key ideas are distilled in his 2015 manual *Copy Copy Copy* which is required reading.

Speaking of hindsight, we've never held much truck with the old Gladwell 'Hush Puppies' story.

The legend goes along these lines; some East Village hipsters began wearing Hush Puppies in 1994 and then, such was their 'influence', everyone else started wearing them, too.

What Gladwell failed to notice is that Hush Puppies were a staple of just about every UK subculture from the early sixties onwards, worn by mods, skins, hippies, punks, soul-boys and ravers.

Right through to 3rd generation mod Brit-poppers like Oasis and Blur in ermm.. about 1994.

Even if Gladwell's theory were true, it still doesn't mean that if East Village hipsters did wear a specific product then it would automatically be popular.

Hipsters in the East Village presumably wear all kinds of other clobber that never becomes particularly popular anywhere else, or even in the East Village.

It depends on whether anyone else was open to copying at that time.

This belief in 'influencers' can be simply explained using a particular kind of logical fallacy, often described as Rosenweig's 'delusion of the wrong end of the stick'.

This is the tendency to get cause and effect the wrong way round.

For instance, in observing that successful companies tend to have a corporate social responsibility policy, should one infer that these pro-social activities are contributing factors to their success, or is it simply that that profitable companies tend to have money to spend on CSR?

The former makes for a better story – and is therefore lapped up by the purpose-before-profit lobby and more recently proponents of the so-called 'sharing economy' - however the latter explanation is much closer to the truth, if somewhat less sexy.

Similarly, 'influencer' theory makes for a better story than random copying of each other by ordinary people.

The final irony is, of course, that the so-called 'traditional' mass marketing that 'influencer' type strategies seeks to discredit is actually far more effective at reaching accidental influencers than activity focused on reaching those with some sort of perceived influence.

Therefore smart marketers could, in effect, have their influencer cake and eat it, too.

As it is impossible to know which person, if any, is going to start any given cascade of influence, then activities should be aimed at as broad a market as possible to give it the best possible chance.

And then if something does catch on they can correctly say 'we got the influencers' because the random nature of accidental influence means that 'influencers' can only really be identified after the fact.

'I'll be your mirror,
Reflect what you are, in case you don't know'

Keep it real

All the world is a stage. And one man in his time plays many parts.

'Rather than seeking primarily to arrive at accurate representations of a common world, the individual turns toward trying to provide honest representations of himself.

It is as though he decides that since it makes no sense to try to be true to the facts, he must therefore try instead to be true to himself.

[But] there is nothing in theory, and certainly nothing in experience, to support the extraordinary judgment that it is the truth about himself that is the easiest for a person to know.

Our natures are, indeed, elusively insubstantial—notoriously less stable and less inherent than the natures of other things.

And insofar as this is the case, sincerity itself is bullshit.'

The above is a shortened version of the closing remarks from Harry G. Frankfurt's famous philosophy essay *On Bullshit,* first published in 1986 and still widely regarded as the closest thing we have to unified theory of bullshit.

'Sincerity itself is bullshit'

Or is it, as some might say, that 'authentic' experience is transformed and then rendered 'inauthentic' by its incorporation into the totality (the all-pervasive supremacy of the whole over the parts) resulting in alienation?

Maybe so, but putting postmodernist gobbledygook to one side, notions of the 'authentic' self do cross over into some of the popular ideas in modern branding and advertising theory.

Marketing experts and commentators continually demand authenticity from brands.

A brand should 'provide honest and authentic representation of itself.'

And if that's not enough, it's claimed in some quarters that these authentic brands should not even be concerned with the grubby business of making a sale!

I'm not sure what industry some of these people think they are in.

It is widely claimed that rather than being simply social and transactional, brands should instead be concerned with seeking a deep connection, engaging on a personal level with the individual. And then saving the world.

And that advertising which attempts to put memorable

campaigns in front of mass audiences with the intention of getting a brand thought of momentarily the next time the consumer wants to buy from the category, is somehow inauthentic.

The commentators who espouse this theory seem very certain that this is the way forward for brands, yet there is scant evidence that any consumers out there even want to engage with brands at all, and even thinking about brands is something that most people spend very little mental energy over.

Returning to Frankfurt's text briefly...

'Bullshit is unavoidable whenever circumstances require someone to talk without knowing what he is talking about.

Thus the production of bullshit is stimulated whenever person's obligations or opportunities to speak about some topic exceed his knowledge of the facts that are relevant to that topic.'

This discrepancy is common in the advertising trade press.

What is authentic, anyway?

Erving Goffman is considered to be perhaps the most influential sociologist of recent times and *The Presentation of Self in Everyday Life* - first published in 1959 - provides a detailed analysis of process and meaning in, what Goffman calls, mundane interaction - ordinary face-to-face interactions among people in various social situations.

Goffman employs the 'dramaturgical approach'. He is principally concerned with the different modes of 'presentation' employed by people and therefore the meaning of each in its social context.

In essence, all human interactions are 'performance', shaped by the environment, the audience, and are constructed in order to provide others with 'impressions' that are consonant with the desired goals of the actor.

According to Goffman, one's social identity is a series of 'fronts'. There is no 'authentic' 'self'. All the world is a stage.

Human social interactions are all performances conducted when on-stage, in social situations.

It may be that no *self* is particularly in charge. In *The Rational Animal* Psychology Professors Douglas Kenrick and Vlad Griskevicius describe a (sometimes) co-operative committee composed of seven key 'subselves' - the modules we talked about earlier - each competing for control and with their own agenda: self-protection, mate attraction, mate retention, affiliation (making alliances), kin care, social status, and disease avoidance etc.

One of our *sub-selves* that will assume command more often than not is the social status seeking *self*. Given that much of the interests of the other *selves* are linked to the success of social status this is unsurprising. People are always competing for status. Products and brands are signifiers of that status.

So, even being anti-consumption is still conspicuous, 'authenticity' is simply the new 'cool' and so even when one attempts to remove oneself from the competition for status in the mainstream you are simply joining the competition for status in a different sphere.

'What? You mean you still actually BUY products? We only share and freecycle'

Thorstein Veblen's *The Theory of the Leisure Class: An Economic Study of Institutions*, published in 1899, is a detailed social critique of 'conspicuous consumption' as a function of social-class consumerism.

Veblen was probably one of the great grandfathers of behavioural economics, and 'Leisure Class' is as good a description of 21st century internet culture as there is - his view of people was generally one of 'irrational creatures who relentlessly pursue social status with little regard to their own happiness'.

When Veblen describes nineteenth-century aristocrats as spending their 'leisure' time fox hunting or learning obscure languages he says; that in order to be successful (as a signal), the signs of this conspicuous display needed to portray themselves as at least superficially useful or socially beneficial.

That is, it needs to pretend to be something other than what it really is. For example, fox hunting as some sort of duty to protect the livelihoods of serfs/farmers.

Or Bono, he has accrued some considerable wealth but - as he is not likely to trouble the pop charts again and therefore bugger-all to do all day - turning up at the UN to save the world is helping to resolve some sort of cognitive dissonance around leisure and offshore investments.

Or imagined socially beneficial properties of the so-called collaborative economy products, which serve only to solve a cognitive dissonance for buyers of those services.

It disguises the real motivation - which is, of course, status seeking. In other words, *conspicuous* authenticity.

When the big supermarkets joined in the 'organic' game a few years back one would have imagined that those who truly believed in the benefits of organic produce would have welcomed this as a good thing.

Now that ordinary shoppers could have access to organic produce then surely that would mean we would all have the opportunity to eat healthier and live in a better environment, right?

But the more organic became available to the mass of

ordinary consumers, the less it is serves as a source of distinction for the status seekers.

Hence the original organic brigade moved on to 'local diet' as the next logical step. Then when that caught-on then 'artisanal' became an expression of more-authentic-than-thou.

In *The Authenticity Hoax*, author Andrew Potter describes a 'basic fusion of the two ideals of the privately beneficial and the morally praiseworthy' as the 'bait-and switch' (or cognitive dissonance) at the heart of the authenticity hoax.'

'This desire for the personal and the public to align explains why so much of what passes for authentic living has a do-gooder spin to it. Yet the essentially status-oriented nature of the activity always reveals itself eventually.'

Fake authenticity solves a cognitive dissonance problem for status-seeking consumers – their anti-consumerism beliefs clash with their regular consumerist behaviours, so using the likes of AirBnB or LeftoverSwap allows them to tell themselves a story about authentic living with a do-gooder spin.

It's the same for advertising professionals who baulk at the crassness of selling.

But Potter kindly hands us a get out of jail card.

'We live in the world of bullshit, but as long as you know it is bullshit, and as long as they know that you know it is bullshit, then it's a game we can all play.'

In his previous book *The Rebel Sell* Potter and co-author Joseph Heath note that 'whenever you look at the list of consumer goods that [according to critics of capitalism] people don't really need, what you invariably see is a list of consumer goods that middle-aged intellectuals don't need ... Hollywood movies bad, performance art good; Chryslers bad, Volvos good; hamburgers bad, risotto good.'

It could even be that 'millennials' - the bullshit-proof authenticity-seeking information generation defined both by their strongly held values and their strong intention to live by them (ugh) - is another invention of these same middle-aged intellectuals, are now looking to temper the disappointment they feel over their own generation's counter-culture failure.

Of course, every new pseudo anti-establishment approach business that declares itself as some sort of alternative to the mainstream - more artisanal, authentic or purpose-driven – is simply a response to demand from the mass market looking for things to consume that signal their alternative status to others.

The best description of anti-consumerism is 'the criticism of what other people buy'.

But the truth is that the market is just as good at meeting

consumer demand for anti-consumer products as it is for straight up consumer products.

In Jean Baudrillard's 1970 *obscuritain* 'classic', *The Consumer Society*, postmodernisms poster-child describes consumption itself as some sort of 'magical thinking'. This is why advertising works so well. The magic of goods conveying properties beyond their intended use.

But the fatal flaw in this 'reasoning' is that anti-consumption is just as magical - probably more so.

Now you can feel like a do-gooder and still consume.

And it is the same old competitive consumption, which drives this same consumer spending.

Consumerism is something we do to each other, and if anything, straight up conspicuous consumption is more authentic than conscious consumption because at least the status-driven nature of it is not disguised.

Sadly, the calls for authentic brands and authentic voices are ultimately futile.

All social interaction is intrinsically inauthentic and performance. In fact the performance itself is the only authenticity.

Maybe impersonal behaviours are far more useful; attempting brand authenticity crosses the streams.

As Dan Ariely has pointed out in *Predictably Irrational*, we live simultaneously in two different worlds.

One where social norms prevail, and the other governed by market norms.

'Social norms are wrapped up in our social nature and our need for community. They are usually warm and fuzzy. Instant paybacks are not required: you may help move your neighbour's couch, but this doesn't mean he has to come right over and move yours.

The second world, the one governed by market norms, is very different. There's nothing warm and fuzzy about it. The exchanges are sharp- edged: wages, prices, rents, interest, and costs- and- benefits.

Such market relationships are not necessarily evil or mean- in fact, they also include self- reliance, inventiveness, and individualism-but they do imply comparable benefits and prompt payments'.

What hope then for brands in finding an 'authentic voice' or being 'authentic'? Or the much trumpeted millennial consumer quest for authenticity? It may be a nice quality to have, but it has nothing to do with solving anyone's washing powder problem.

When a mysterious and previously unlisted Picasso painting fell into the hands of one of his most serious (bourgeois) collectors, the lucky enthusiast took it to the artist himself in order that Pablo could authenticate the piece in person.

Picasso took one look at the painting and declared it an imposter.

Not to be deterred, the hapless collector purchased another piece and, again, took this to the artist for authentication.

Picasso again declared that the piece was a fake.

In a last ditch attempt our collector commissioned a bespoke work, and then proceeded to watch over Picasso himself as he made the painting, in order that he could be sure of its authenticity, by witnessing its creation with his own eyes. But upon completion, Picasso yet again declared the new painting to be a fake.

The puzzled collector protested 'But I saw you paint this one with my own eyes'.

To which the deadpan Pablo replied 'I can paint a fake Picasso better than anyone'.

And so Pablo Picasso was never called an asshole.

Have a nice day.

Never mind the Baldricks

Pedantic, expensive and subversive.

In 1968, Stanley Pollitt, along with Martin Boase and Gabe Massimi, opened the doors of their new agency, imaginatively named, Boase Massimi Pollitt.

The three of them had worked at Interpublic agency Pritchard-Wood & Partners.

(No relation, as far as I know, however if anyone out there with the surname Wood wants to start an agency give me a shout.)

BMP emerged after the trio had un-successfully attempted a management buy-out of Pritchard-Wood and, instead, started up their own agency.

It was while at BMP that Stanley Pollitt was able to fully form *his* vision of the Account Planning function.

I say 'his' vision because, coincidentally, one Stephen King over at JWT was having similar ideas at the same time.

Now, the pair are almost universally recognised as the godfathers of the discipline. Here's Pollitt's early description of the emergent account planner.

'The account planner is that member of the agency's team who is the expert, through background, training, experience, and attitudes, at working with information and getting it used - not just marketing research but all the information available to help solve a client's advertising problems'.

For the 'expert' that Pollitt describes, his or her single most important task was to get the advertising 'right' and both Pollitt and King advocated an approach based less on gut feel and more on scientific foundation.

Or, at least, a kind of *inductive* reasoning.

I mention this as Pollitt and King came to mind while contemplating the following passage from Pinker's *How The Mind Works.*

Pinker is making the distinction between proper science versus *pseudo*science. He could just as easily be making the case for proper strategy as opposed to *pseudo* strategy.

Psuedo strategy represents the activities undertaker by the proliferation of 'experts' in the now greatly expanded realm of fluff and gibberish that passes for 'strategy' of some shape or form in agencies.

(The principal skill of many of these strategists being the ability to 'find the data' that promotes their particular case and specialism. The answer is [insert specialism], now what's the question?) In any case, data (good or bad) is *made* not *found*.

Pinker explains:

'Experts are invaluable and are usually rewarded in esteem and wealth. But our reliance on experts puts temptation in their path. The experts can allude to a world of wonders - occult forces, angry gods, and magical potions - that is inscrutable to mere mortals but reachable through their services.

Tribal shamans are flimflam artists who supplement their considerable practical knowledge with stage magic, drug-induced trances, and other cheap tricks. In a complex society, a dependence on experts leaves us even more vulnerable to quacks, from carnival snake-oil salesman to the mandarins who advise governments to adopt programs implemented by mandarins.

Good science is pedantic, expensive, and subversive.'

Dictionary.com appears to have a different view of 'pedantic', their description given is as follows:

'The nit-pickery of the English language that drives the less detail oriented insane...often mistaken as a tool to impress others when in fact it is annoying.'

For planning to get the advertising 'right' perhaps some nit-pickery is a necessary risk. I've mapped Pinker's *trifecta* onto the three critical factors that Stanley Pollitt decreed to be essential for effective account planning.

Pedantic – 'This means total agency management commitment to getting the advertising content right at all costs. This means creating effective advertising instead of focusing on maximising profits or keeping the clients happy.'

Expensive – 'The agency commits the resources to allow planners to be more than temporary role players. Account planners must be given the leeway to work with the data and research as they see fit.'

Subversive – 'It means changing some of the basic ground rules. Once consumer response becomes the most important element in making final advertising judgments, it makes many of the more conventional means of judgment sound hollow.'

As an interesting footnote, and whilst poking around for some other Pollitt related nuggets, we were naturally delighted to find that aside from the great man's contribution to establishing the account planning discipline in the advertising industry he also made a major contribution to the popular culture (and the punk canon in particular).

His daughter, Tessa, was the bass player in The Slits.

Sadly, Stanley died just as The Slits were taking off. Despite being present on the punk scene since '76 it was not until 1979 that their debut album *Cut* appeared. I'm not certain he would have liked the banging and shouting.

Pollitt (and King) would, almost certainly, have had no time at all for the tribal shamans and flimflam artists known as marketing gurus.

The word guru has its origins in Sanskrit, the primary liturgical language of Hinduism.

Much can be learned from ancient eastern wisdom. Not least a healthy scepticism of the self-anointed thought-leader or guru.

The *Kularnava Tantra* is an important text of the Shakta Agamic tantra tradition and of Hindu spiritual thought, and includes this nugget.

'There are many gurus who may rob the disciple's wealth but few who can remove the disciple's affliction.'

Indeed, the Dunning-Kruger Effect - which weaves itself throughout this book - also has its roots in another ancient text.

'A fool who knows his foolishness is wise at least to that extent, but a fool who thinks himself wise is a fool indeed.'

From The *Dhammapada*, circa 4th century BCA.

But really this book has been about a kind of economics, and for the sake of argument, let's accept the Lionel Robbins definition of modern economics. Robbins was chair of the London School of Economics in the early 30's and was also influential in the expansion of the British University system in the 60's and a voice for government funding of the Arts at the same time. Not a bad chap for an economist.

'Economics is the science which studies human behaviour as a relationship between ends and scarce means which have alternative uses.'

People want more of what there is less of; therefore that resource which is in scarce supply can command more value.

This should mean good news for the supplier of the scarce resource. But 'content' is not scarce, media is not scarce and nor are the gurus.

The democratisation of the production and distribution of media afforded by the internet is not in doubt. The fact that any form of media one can imagine is being produced in huge volumes by millions of people is also a given.

So, while there may be millions of people able to produce media in any given format for any platform the sheer ubiquitousness means that in economic terms it has less value. Particularly if it's being made by monkeys.

There's a scene from the TV show *Mad Men* that I occasionally use in pep talks. In this scene the aspiring copywriter Peggy Olsen presents one of her early campaign ad concepts to Don Draper. A couple are embracing in a print ad for an airline.

'Sex sells', explains Peggy.

Incredulous, Don replies: 'Says who?' Just so you know, the people who talk that way think that monkeys can do this…but they can't do what we do, and they hate us for it.'

Everything changes, everything stays the same. These days one can't walk five yards down the street without bumping into a gaggle of assorted 'content strategists', 'authentic creators', and 'influencers'.

The Dunning-Krugerati. All hail the rise of the idiots!

They can't do what we do, and they hate us for it.

So, where did it all go wrong?

As we set out at the beginning of this book, a *proto-meme* is beginning to 'go critical'. If you've made it this far you are probably part of that meme. Somewhere the advertising business kinda lost the plot, we're just not sure exactly where.

So many incompetents, who can't know we are incompetent because the skills we need to produce the right answers are exactly the skills we lack in order to know what a right answer is.

What happens now?

Dan Gilbert famously observed 'Human beings are works in progress that mistakenly think they're finished.'

Let's hope the advertising industry isn't 'finished' (while some of us are still mistaken in our belief that its a work in progress.)

—₩—

London, the year is 2023 and we are inside the Canary Wharf global headquarters of Blackadder & Partners - the advertising giants recently acquired by uber-holding company WPPwC.

Managing Partner and Global Chief Solutions Imagineer, Blackadder is giving a short history lesson to the young Customer Paradigm Co-coordinator, Baldrick.

Blackadder: 'You see, Baldrick, back in 2017 brands developed omni-channel frameworks to leverage networks of micro influencers with socially created brand equity. The idea being that post-platform data unification would engage millennials with digestible content. That way, the purpose-driven brands of the future would become authentic facilitators in a hyper-connected digital world'.

Baldrick: 'Except, consumers just wanted to buy stuff and get on with their lives?'

Blackadder: 'There was one tiny flaw in the plan.'

Baldrick: 'Oh, what was that?'

Blackadder: 'It was bollocks.'

About the author

Eaon Pritchard has worked as an advertising creative and planner for over 20 years firstly in London and now in Melbourne, Australia.

He also lectures and consults, currently serving on the communications advisory board for RMIT University in Melbourne and writes regularly for WARC and other industry publications.

This is his first book, but there's another one coming.

To have Eaon come and speak to your group or conference email him at eaonspeaking@gmail.com - and have your credit card details to hand.

65060461R00125

Made in the USA
Middletown, DE
22 February 2018